John Gibson Cazenove

St. Hilary of Poitiers and St. Martin of Tours

John Gibson Cazenove

St. Hilary of Poitiers and St. Martin of Tours

ISBN/EAN: 9783337188887

Printed in Europe, USA, Canada, Australia, Japan

Cover: Foto ©Lupo / pixelio.de

More available books at **www.hansebooks.com**

The Fathers for English Readers.

ST. HILARY OF POITIERS

AND

ST. MARTIN OF TOURS.

BY

JOHN GIBSON CAZENOVE, D.D.

SUB-DEAN AND CHANCELLOR OF ST. MARY'S CATHEDRAL, EDINBURGH.

PUBLISHED UNDER THE DIRECTION OF THE TRACT COMMITTEE.

LONDON:
SOCIETY FOR PROMOTING CHRISTIAN KNOWLEDGE,
NORTHUMBERLAND AVENUE, CHARING CROSS, W.C. ;
43, QUEEN VICTORIA STREET, E.C. ;
26, ST. GEORGE'S PLACE, HYDE PARK CORNER, S.W.
BRIGHTON: 135, NORTH STREET.
NEW YORK: E. & J. B. YOUNG & CO.
1883.

PREFACE.

THE biographies contained in this small volume are based, like the rest of the series, upon a study of the original authorities. These are, in the case of St. Hilary, most especially the very considerable writings which he has left us. In the case of St. Martin, we have to depend almost exclusively upon the comparatively small treatises of Sulpicius Severus; for St. Gregory of Tours, though greatly extolling him, tells us hardly anything concerning Martin's earthly career, and the poems of Paulinus of Perigueux and of Venantius Fortunatus are little more than reproductions in verse of the prose narrative of the earlier biographer.

It is right to confess my obligations to the authors cited in the notes, not only for the particular information therein mentioned, but also for much general light upon the topics discussed   Let me add a word of gratitude, for what are sometimes called side-lights, to Dean Merivale's " History of the Romans under the Empire"; to " Les Césars " of Count Franz de Champagny; to the " Heathenism and Judaism " and to " The First Age of the Church " of Dr. Von Döllinger; and to the Commentary of Bishop

Lightfoot on the Epistle of St. Paul to the Colossians. I have also made free use, sometimes for elucidation, sometimes for confirmation of conclusions reached independently, of the "Dictionary of Christian Biography" which is in progress under the editorship of Dr. William Smith and Professor Wace; more particularly of the articles on *Damasus* and *Liberius*, and of my own contributions on *Hilarius Pictaviensis* and *Martinus Turonensis*.

The very mixed character of the Emperor Maximus is coloured with a more romantic tint than is discernible in the pages of Sulpicius and of the pagan historian Pacatus in the poem entitled "The Dream of Maxen Wledig," which forms one of "The Visions of England" depicted for us by Mr. Francis Palgrave. The fact that the poem is inspired by "The Mabinogion," the collection of the legends of that highly poetic country, Wales, may suffice to account for the apparent discrepancy. If any of my readers are induced to compare the two portraits, they may perhaps be inclined to think that of the Latin historians the more probable. But in any case they will, if I mistake not, feel grateful for the reference to a book which, over and above its poetic merits, is so full of instruction and suggestiveness to all students of history.

J. G. C.

EDINBURGH,
Midsummer, 1883.

CONTENTS.

ST. HILARY OF POITIERS.

ST. MARTIN OF TOURS.

CHAPTER VIII.

CHAPTER IX.

CHAPTER X.

ST. HILARY OF POITIERS.

CHAPTER I.

THE COUNTRY AND THE AGE OF HILARY.

It was permitted by God's providence that at the time when His Son, for us men and for our salvation, came down from heaven, heathen Rome should be the mistress of the world. But to reach this pinnacle of earthly greatness had been a long and arduous task—a task achieved by hard-won triumphs against able and often formidable enemies.

Among the opponents of the pre-eminence of Rome, the Gauls were for many centuries the most uncompromising. Their opposition, it is true, was of a wayward and fitful character. The different tribes of the race did not often act in concert; and, even when they did so, their harmony was soon broken. No Gallic general can be said to have attained the high position won by Pyrrhus of Epirus, far less that achieved by Hannibal, in a career of anti-Roman warfare. Even Brennus, the chieftain of the Gauls, who in B.C. 390 captured and burnt Rome, did not remain in central Italy long enough to consolidate his conquest.

B

But while the rivalry of other enemies, as of the Epirote and the Carthaginian, was comprised within a comparatively limited period of time, that of the Gauls was enduring and persistent. The Celtic tribes in that part of northern Italy which the Romans called Cisalpine Gaul, as well as those who occupied so large a portion of the country now known to us as France, continued for more than three centuries to be the watchful and unsleeping foes of Rome. They looked out for opportunities, and when they saw them were not very scrupulous about breach of treaties. The sudden and irregular character of the Celtic attacks was of that kind which the Romans specified by the name of *a tumult;* and, as a Gallic tumult was an event which might happen at any moment, a special fund of money was kept in the Temple of Saturn in order to meet such an emergency.

A day, however, was to come when the long duel between these powers was doomed to cease. Cisalpine Gaul was humbled and reduced to a Roman province about B.C. 200, soon after the defeat of Hannibal. About 150 years later that remarkable man, who has been justly called the greatest and most versatile of all Romans, Caius Julius Cæsar, in a series of campaigns, which lasted for nine years, completely subdued the whole of the Further Gaul. We must not pause to consider the character and the motives of the conqueror. But it seems only fair to remark, that when it is asserted, and perhaps truly, that a million of Gauls may have perished in fighting against Cæsar, it is a mere assumption to imply, as is often done, that these warriors would have died a natural

death if they had escaped the sword of Rome. With
the exception of those who had been civilised by
the influence of the Roman province in the south-
east (the district subsequently known as Provence),
the inhabitants of Gaul were a nation of fighters,
and the men struck down by Cæsar would have
perished in domestic feuds or in some of their almost
daily battles with the Germans. That this great feat
did subserve the further plans of the ambitious conqueror is, of course, quite undeniable. No part of
Cæsar's career seems to have produced a deeper impression on the imagination of the Roman people.
The treasure preserved in the Saturnian temple was
appropriated by Cæsar on the occasion of his trium-
phant entry into Rome, in B.C. 49, after he had
crossed the Rubicon. To the protest of the tribune,
Metellus, that it was a deed of sacrilege to touch this
fund for any purpose except to repel a Gallic invasion,
Cæsar was able to make the swift and proud retort,
" the fear of a Gallic invasion is for ever at an end ;
I have subdued the Gauls."

From that date Gaul not merely accepted the yoke
of Rome, but enlisted her sons in Roman armies, and
eagerly studied Roman literature and Roman law.
Cæsar, with that wondrous power of fascination
which he exerted alike over friends and foes, raised a
legion composed of his former adversaries, which
bore a lark upon its helmets and was known, from the
Celtic name for that bird, as the *Legio Alauda*. Under
the rule of Augustus, the quickness of the native
Gallic intellect displayed itself in an eager adaptation
of the language and the arts of their conquerors. Six

or seven cities became famous for military manufactures, such as the red cloth worn by Roman soldiers. Medicine and philosophy were likewise sedulously cultivated, but of all studies rhetoric was among the most popular. The contests of the bar especially delighted the litigious and loquacious spirit of the Gauls. Arles, Toulouse, and Vienne were conspicuous as seats of classic literature ; Lyons was celebrated, as a Roman biographer and satirist inform us,[1] for its rhetorical contests ; and the Latinity of Gaul, though somewhat deficient in that severity of taste which marked the style of the best models in Rome, yet often undoubtedly displayed a character of really rich and copious eloquence.

The contest at Lyons embraced both Greek and Latin composition. Marseilles, believed to have been founded by Greeks, was esteemed to be the headquarters of Grecian culture in Gaul ; and traces of some knowledge of Greek remained for four or five centuries in the south-eastern part of the country.

The above facts will be found to bear upon the next great event in the history of the country ; an event of far more importance than even its conquest by Cæsar ; although, humanly speaking, that conquest was its necessary prelude. We refer to the introduction of the Christian religion into the land. The Christian faith must have penetrated Gaul at least as early as A.D. 170 ; for by A.D. 177 we find a religious colony from Asia Minor or Phrygia settled on the

---

[1] Suetonius, "Life of Caligula," sec. 20; Juvenal, "Satires," i., line 44.

banks of the river Rhone, and keeping up in the Greek language a correspondence with the mother Church in the Eastern clime from which it sprang. The occasion of this correspondence was a terrible but a very glorious one. The philosophic Stoic, the last of that school, the virtuous Marcus Aurelius, was then seated on the imperial throne. But this emperor, though he may not have originated the fearful persecution of the Christians which broke out at Lyons and at Vienne, virtually encouraged it by the rescript which he addressed to the local authorities. The fearful details of the cruelties exercised upon the sufferers, and the constancy with which they were borne, have been powerfully narrated by many modern historians. But it is not easy to surpass the simple pathos of the original letter preserved for us in the pages of Eusebius.[1] Here it must suffice to remind the reader, as a proof of the way in which all ranks were blended by their common faith, that while the aged Bishop of Lyons, Potheinus, who perished in that persecution, was a man of station and culture, yet its heroine, the greatest sufferer of all, was the lowly Christian slave, Blandina.

Gaul had already proved a fruitful soil for the spread of the new creed. This violent persecution, so nobly met, greatly intensified its power, and afforded a new illustration of the often-quoted maxim of Tertullian, " The blood of martyrs is the seed of the Church." During the succeeding century the Christians of Gaul,

[1] Eusebius, "Ecclesiastical History," book v., chap. i. A short extract is given in a volume of this series, "Defenders of the Faith," by the Rev. F. Watson, M.A., p. 17.

though always liable to outbursts of popular fury,
appear to have enjoyed comparative tranquillity.

But the latest and fiercest of the persecutions
(which broke out in A.D. 303 and lasted for nearly ten
years), the one commanded by the Emperor Diocletian,
at the instigation of his colleague Galerius, embraced
in its wide range alike the most eastern provinces of
the empire and the western province of Gaul. Happily
the governor, Constantius Chlorus, was not only of
a mild and tolerant disposition, but also cherished in
his inmost heart a very great respect for Christians.
He was compelled, indeed, for the sake of appearances, to do something. The overthrow of a few
churches, which had already been much damaged,
and the forcible closing of some others marked the
extent of his interference. Not only did he refrain
from any cruelties towards persons, but he acted in a
way which showed the value which he placed upon
consistency. Summoning to his presence those among
his officers who made a profession of Christianity,
he inquired of them what would be their conduct,
if he should find himself obliged to enforce the
imperial decrees, and to call upon those around him
to offer sacrifice, or at least incense to the heathen
gods. Some of them announced that, though such a
proceeding would be most painful to their feelings,
they would not like to disobey the emperor, and were
prepared to yield the point. Others declared, however much they might regret finding themselves
placed in such a dilemna, nothing should induce them
to render homage to the pagan deities. The governor
dismissed them without any remark. But, somewhat

to the surprise of both sets, it was soon found that promotion and places of trust were bestowed, not upon those who had expressed their willingness to yield, but upon those who had avowed their inability so to act. Constantius explained to private friends, that he could not confide in the loyalty professed towards an earthly master by men so ready to betray Him whom they professed to regard as a heavenly one.

Constantius Chlorus, who for two years (A.D. 305–6) ruled as emperor conjointly with Galerius, died at York, in the imperial palace of that city, in A.D. 306. We are not surprised to learn that under his tolerant rule Christianity had made considerable progress in Gaul, and that by the close of the fourth century there were not less than twenty bishoprics in this important province. The Gaul of that date, it may be observed in passing, was rather more extensive than the France of our own days, and constituted as much as one-twelfth part of the mighty Roman empire. Constantius was succeeded by his son, Constantine, the first emperor who made a public profession of Christianity and mounted the cross upon the imperial diadem. That the symbol of agony and shame should be thus exalted in the sight of men was the outward mark of a vast revolution—a revolution alike in the world of thought and of action—a revolution social and political as well as spiritual.

The motives and the character of Constantine were mixed. He remained, both as a politician and in his domestic affairs, cold, and too often cruel. He put

to death his rival, Licinius, in A.D. 322, not wholly
perhaps without excuse, but still in such wise as to
lay himself open to the charge of bad faith.   A few
years later he also executed his own son, Crispus,
whom he believed to have conspired against him.
But the subsequent conviction that Crispus was either
innocent, or at least less guilty than had been supposed, led Constantine into furious indignation against
his second wife, Fausta, who had been the chief
accuser of her stepson.   Accordingly, Fausta also
was put to death, as, what heathens would have called,
a sacrifice to the manes of Crispus.

If deeds of this nature had been committed by a
heathen emperor, they would have excited comparatively little attention ; but that one who professed
himself a Christian should thus act has, not unnaturally, drawn down upon Constantine's memory
far severer comments, most especially from the
heathen annalists of his reign, Zosimus and Aurelius
Victor.   For our part, we gladly adopt on this subject the observations of an historian of our day :—
" We must frankly admit that Constantine, who
yet warred with the faith of a Christian, and often
conducted his government in accordance with the
light shed by the Gospel, nevertheless, avenged his
private wrongs with the rigour, and often with the
cunning, of a Roman emperor of the old creed. History has a right to notify, in his case, with astonishment and severity, vices which were familiar to his
predecessors. *It is one additional mark of homage
which she renders to his character and his faith.*"[1]

[1] Duc de Broglie.

From the same historian we borrow the following masterly and candid summary of the general character of the chief human agent in that great revolution, which embraced in its operations the important province of Gaul. He observes, that before we answer the question whether Constantine, in his conversion, was actuated by shrewd political calculation or by a feeling of true faith, we must determine what we mean by faith. Of that sincere and living faith which is associated with penitent compunction, amendment of life, conquest of passions, detachment from the prizes of earth, Constantine had but a very imperfect grasp until his death-bed sickness. He remained ambitious, and was (as we have observed) too often cruel. But to admit thus much is very different from saying that Constantine did not really believe and reverence the Christian religion. The acceptance of Christianity by a sovereign far from being, on merely human grounds, a sure road to power, was a great risk. It alienated more than half his subjects from him; it snapped the link with all the memorials and traditions of the empire; it involved him in very serious political embarrassments. Even the hesitating manner in which he interfered with the internal discussions of the Church betokened his scrupulousness; for in matters of state he was accustomed to command without debating. With all these pledges of conscientious conviction before us, it seems impossible for impartial judges to doubt the sincerity of Constantine.

" The glory of men is for the most part increased by the importance of the events with which they are mixed up, and more than one famous name has thus owed its celebrity to a fortuitous combination. But the destiny of Constantine has been precisely the reverse of this. In his case, on the contrary, it is the greatness of the work which dims the reputation of the workman. Between the results of his reign and his personal merits there is by no means the ordinary proportion between cause and effect. To be worthy of attaching his name to the conversion of the world he needed to have joined to the genius of heroes the virtues of saints. Constantine was neither great enough nor pure enough for his task. The contrast, but too manifest to all eyes, has justly shocked posterity. *Nevertheless, history has seen so few sovereigns devote to the service of a noble cause their power, and even their ambition, that it has a right, when it meets with such, to demand for them the justice of men and to hope for the mercy of God.*"[1]

Constantine, whose acceptance of Christianity put a stop to all further persecution from heathens (save during the brief episode of the reign of his grandson, Julian the Apostate), died in A.D. 337, having first moved the seat of empire from Rome to the famous city on the Bosphorus, which is still called after him, Constantinople. The empire, as many of our readers will remember, was divided among his three sons— Constans, Constantius, and Constantine II. Gibbon's judgment on their capacities for swaying the rod of empire is well known. He ranks in this respect a celebrated ecclesiastical leader (though from the

---

[1] De Broglie, "L'Église et l'Empire au Quatrième Siècle,' tome ii., p. 130. Paris, 1856.

sceptical historian's point of view "his mind was tainted by the contagion of fanaticism") far above all three : "Athanasius displayed a superiority of character and abilities which would have qualified him far better than the degenerate sons of Constantine for the government of a great monarchy."[1] This threefold rule did not long endure. Before three years had passed away, Constantine, making war upon Constans, was defeated and put to death. For ten years (340–50) Constans and Constantius were joint emperors; but in A.D. 350 Constans was slain by Magnentius, and then Constantius in turn, slaying the usurper, became sole emperor, and ruled the provinces formerly under the authority of his brothers.

The condition, then, of the Gaul of the fourth century was that of a large province of a mighty empire, which had derived a portion indeed of its earlier intellectual culture from Greece, but which was now organised on Roman principles in all that concerned its temporal government. The system of taxation of the public domains, of roads traversed by imperial posts, of enlistment and management of the army, was all administered from Rome. Some few judicial and municipal liberties were left ; but even these were falling more and more under the influence of the central authority. At the time of which we speak, these institutions, which were pagan in their origin, remained essentially such ; for not only were large tracts of Gaul un-Christianised, but even in the Christian parts society had not been in any wise

---

[1] " Decline and Fall," chap. xxi.

leavened by Christian principle. Nevertheless, there
existed among the Christian portions a freedom of
thought and of action unknown among the function-
aries of the civil administration. The civil authorities
were jealously watched from Rome, but the rulers
of the Christian society were (excepting in times of
persecution) left very much to themselves. It will
be seen, however, from the following narrative that
Constantius acted in this respect differently from
former emperors.

Meanwhile, the progress of Christianity had been
troubled by something worse perhaps than heathen
persecution. The heresy of Arius—that is to say,
the denial of the central truth of the Christian faith,
the full divinity of Christ,—had by this time spread
into Gaul, and had been adopted by some even
among the bishops of the Church. The favour of
the court was also largely extended towards it.

Such was the Gaul of the fourth century, in which
Hilary's lot was cast. To what extent the Celtic
blood permeated ancient Gaul is a question much
disputed. But it was certainly the *dominant* race.
Different tribes of this family had often a capital
town, which in time lost its prior name, and was
called by the name of the clan. Thus, for example,
the city which in Cæsar's " Commentaries " is *Lutetia*
of the *Parisii* became Paris ; *Avaricum* of the *Bitu-
riges* became Bourges ; and Hilary's home, once
called *Limonum* of the *Pictones* or *Pictavienses*, at an
early period became *Pictavi*, and thence *Poictiers* or
Poitiers.

CHAPTER II.

OUTLINES OF THE CAREER OF HILARY.

THERE are three questions to which we expect some manner of reply when we take up the biography of any man of note. In the first place, we desire to ask, What were the outward facts of his career? Secondly, what was the influence of his age upon him? Thirdly, what was his influence upon his age? In the case before us, the answer to the last of these questions must be gathered from our narrative and criticisms taken as a whole. But some reply to the first, and even partially to the second, of these queries may be briefly given here, although they will be treated with greater fulness in the course of our succeeding chapters.

The outward facts of Hilary's career may be summarily stated as follows :—He was born in or near Poitiers in the early part of the fourth century. We do not know the exact date, but it may probably have been between A.D. 315 and 320. The parents of Hilary were pagans, people of high station, who gave their son an excellent education. While still a young man, he became a Christian. He married, and had one child, a daughter, by name Abra. In A.D. 353 he was elected, while yet a layman, to the see of his native town. As bishop he contended earnestly against Arianism in Gaul. Three years later we find him exiled to Phrygia by the emperor. There, too, he did his best, by writings and by influence in councils, to struggle against Arians, but at the same time to make peace, if possible, with the semi-Arians. He found time to compose commentaries on parts of Holy Scripture, and a treatise on the Holy Trinity. In A.D. 360, after an exile of more than three years, he was allowed to return home. He did not, however, reach Poitiers until the year 362, when he rejoined his wife and daughter. In A.D. 364 he made a journey into Italy to confront the then bishop of Milan, Auxentius, whom he regarded as hypocritical. In the year following he returned to Poitiers, and died there peacefully in A.D. 368.

In an earlier period of the Church's history, Hilary's courage and outspokenness would probably have enrolled him among the martyrs put to death by heathen rulers. In the later middle age he might possibly have remained a layman, and tried to interpenetrate judicial or political duties with Christian principles. But he was born too late for the struggle against heathen persecutions, and too soon for the attempt to Christianise the work of a statesman. His friends and neighbours showed a true instinct when they selected him for the office of a bishop, although they could not have foreseen the deep and far-reaching penetration of his future influence.

Whether Hilary did not, like many good men, see but too keenly the evils of his own times, and fancy that the former days had been better than they really were ; whether he fully realised the power of those good influences around him which co-operated with holier aids to save him from the falsities, first of heathenism and then of heresy, may be doubted. But it will be seen, that the very perils and trials, arising out of the temper and circumstances of the age in which his lot was cast, brought out the nobler elements of his character ; and that, though he may have been betrayed into excess of denunciation of at least one adversary, he deservedly earned, alike by his charity and firmness, the honourable title of "Confessor," bestowed on those who struggled for the faith, though they may not have been called upon to resist even unto blood.

CHAPTER III.

THE YOUTH OF HILARY.

HILARY is one of those men whose writings, though they cannot fairly be charged with egotism, yet do tell us a good deal about himself. His largest, perhaps his most important work, the treatise on " The Holy Trinity," composed during his exile in Phrygia, supplies considerable information respecting his youth.

His parents, as we have said, were pagans ; nor do we know whether in their later day they followed the example of their son in embracing Christianity. But they gave him the best education, which they could obtain for him in the Western Gaul, of their time. This education, if we may judge from results, must probably have included some tincture of logic and of mental philosophy. It evidently embraced also a certain measure of acquaintance with Greek, and, above all, with rhetoric, and with the Latin language and literature. Hilary became in time a deep thinker; and, if his powers of expression are not always found adequate to his powers of thought, some allowance must be made for the difficulty of the subjects which he treats, and the inferiority of the Latin to the Greek language in the enunciation of those problems which arise out of philosophy and theology..

A severe critic, belonging to the period of the Reformation, the celebrated Erasmus, pronounces

Hilary somewhat deficient in simplicity and severity of style. Erasmus admits, however, that these gifts were seldom acquired by any writers of Latin, except those who were native Romans, or who had resided from their youth upwards within the city of Rome. There is, no doubt, some ground for this criticism. Indeed, it had been partially anticipated by St. Jerome. Even when that Father of the Church calls Hilary " the Rhone of eloquence," he was, probably, suggesting the idea of a stream, which is often turbid as well as swift and impetuous. Indeed, in another passage Jerome complains of Hilary's periods as being often too lengthy, and, consequently, unintelligible to any but learned readers.

Endued with a temperament which seems to have been by nature lofty, and possessed of no mean amount of intellectual culture, Hilary, while yet a very young man, yearned for knowledge of another kind. He longed to know what was the source, and what the end, of all his thought and action. Merely to enjoy the ease and plenty which his station in life afforded him was to rise but little, if at all, above the brute creation around him. But he must, he felt, be intended for something which was beyond their reach. For example, the desire to attain to truth was in itself a pledge of superiority over the animals. Then there was also the attempt to cherish what all, even among the wiser heathen, admitted to be virtues ; such as, for instance, courage and temperance. With these Hilary learnt to class, he tells us, the passive graces, such as patience and gentleness. But was it to be supposed that all these

energies of the head and of the heart were to cease
with the ending of this life? He could not think so.
A future life to come, at least as happy as that of
earth, in all probability much more so, seemed to
him a natural conclusion of a career of goodness
upon earth. Now such a prize could come from
one source only—namely, from a Supreme Being.
The very notion of "gods many and lords many,"
the error known as polytheism, had always appeared
to him a manifest absurdity.

Let us pause here for a moment. We are all, in
some degree, the creatures of our age. We are all,
in a measure, influenced by what surrounds us. But
this is an influence of which we are only partially
conscious. Hilary, as we have already implied, does
not seem to have suspected how much he may have
been indebted to the atmosphere of thought around
him. His appreciation of the gentler and passive
forms of virtue is unpagan. The same must be said
respecting his perception of the absurdities involved'
in the heathen recognition of many gods. It *is*
absurd; for no one of such beings can really be
God. One of the great attributes of a really Supreme
Being is almightiness,—the possession of a power
which is unlimited, save by His goodness, or by
laws in the world of intellect which He has made
and constituted as part of Himself.[1] But the heathen,

[1] "God, that cannot lie."—Titus i. 2.

> Those transcendent truths
> Of the pure intellect, that stand as laws
> (Submission constituting strength and power)
> Even to Thy Being's infinite majesty!
>   WORDSWORTH, "Excursion," book iv.

as a rule, did not perceive this absurdity. They read in Homer, how a goddess favoured Ulysses and Diomed to the extent of letting them obtain the mystic horses of Rhesus, but how Apollo at this point woke up and prevented them from taking the chariot. Or they learnt from his imitator, Virgil, how Æolus, god of the winds, let loose the gales to please Juno, but was sternly rebuked by Neptune when these breezes made a storm upon the ocean. That Hilary was struck by the incongruities of such a system was most probably owing to a fact repeated in all ages, the indirect impression made by move-ments in the world of thought upon those who do not consciously support or sympathise with such movements. Most justly has Dean Merivale re-marked of Christianity, even in its earliest age, that "when it counted its converts by thousands its unconscious disciples were millions."

Reason and conscience, aided by the atmosphere of thought around him, had led Hilary thus far. But he now began to feel the need of something more, to experience the truth of what, many cen-turies after, was to be expressed by a celebrated English poet:—

> Dim, as the borrow'd beams of moon and stars
> To lonely, weary, wandering travellers,
> Is reason to the soul; and as on high
> Those rolling fires discover but the sky,
> Not light us here, so reason's glimmering ray
> Was lent, not to assure our doubtful way,
> But guide us upward to a better day.[1]

---

[1] Dryden, "Religio Laici."

Happily for Hilary the means of attaining to this better day were accessible.   He was able to obtain and to study the Holy Scriptures ; the Old Testament, probably in the famous Greek translation known as that of the Seventy (the Septuagint), made at Alexandria at least two full centuries before the Christian era ; and the New Testament in the original language.   However imperfect and unequal the Septuagint version may be, it was a mighty instrument in the way of preparing the world for the spread of the Gospel.   Hilary found in the books of Moses and in the Psalms abundant assistance in his desire to know God.

But this knowledge was not unmixed with fear. He was deeply conscious of much weakness, both in the body and in the spirit ; and the thought of the Creator in relation to His creatures was one of reverential awe, as well as love.   There came in, for his consolation and guidance, the books of the new dispensation.   The works of Apostles and Evangelists supplied what the Law and the Prophets could not give.   Hilary was especially drawn to the Gospel of St. John.   Its clear and emphatic language in the Incarnation of the Eternal Son was, to his mind, eminently encouraging and satisfactory.

It need not surprise us to find, that one who had thus mastered the leading principles of true religion, both natural and revealed, should desire to enrol himself as a member of that community with which he was already identified in heart.   About A.D. 350, as nearly as we can make out—in other words, about the middle of the fourth century—Hilary formally renounced paganism, proclaimed himself a Christian, and was thereupon duly baptised.

There are other questions connected with this change which we should be glad to answer if we could. For example, Hilary, at the time of his conversion to Christianity though still tolerably young, was already married and had an infant daughter.

Was his wife a Christian by birth, and had her influence and example anything to do with his change of creed? We cannot say. But such evidence as we do possess seems to render it probable that she was not. Hilary appears to be a very honest writer, and far from reticent in his disclosing the circumstances of his life or his feelings wherever he sees any reason for proclaiming them. Some six years after his conversion, he was doomed to a separation of nearly six years from both wife and daughter. No correspondence between him and them has come down to us, saving one letter to the daughter, who was named Abra. The reference to his wife in this letter (we are ignorant of her name) is tender and respectful. But, if she had been an agent in reclaiming him from heathenism, it would probably have been noticed somewhere, either by Hilary or by those who have furnished us with the materials for his biography.

Did his wife become a Christian at the same time with her husband? Here, again, we lack definite information. But we may almost safely assume that she did. The daughter was evidently nurtured in the faith from the earliest time that she could remember.

For the next three years of his life, Hilary lived as
a good and devout Christian layman. His example
was a thoroughly edifying one to those around him.
On one point he saw reasons, in after-years, to change
his habits. This point was what would now be called
a question of casuistry. Those Holy Scriptures,
which had been his guide to truth, and, under Providence, the chief means of his conversion, seemed to
him at first to inculcate the greatest possible separation, in all 'matters of social intercourse, from Jews
and from heretics. Hilary, in his later days, relaxed
the severity of his rules in this respect. His experience
of life taught him, that by meeting with those who
held false or erroneous doctrines he gained opportunities of influencing them for good. Sometimes a
process, which ended in conversion to the true faith
of Christ, was thus commenced ; and in other cases
he was at least able to soften and to conciliate
opponents.

By casuistry in its good and proper sense—it has
often been abused and so got an ill name—is meant
the application of the general principles of religion
and morality to individual cases, more especially to
cases of apparent difficulty. `Neither of the courses
pursued by Hilary can be called wrong. Each case
must be judged on its own merits. There are men,
who are conscious that such intercourse as Hilary at
first shunned either irritates them, or else leads them
into dangerous concessions. They do well to avoid
the temptation, and they can plead many Scriptural
examples and precepts on their side. Such passages
as the Second Epistle of the loved disciple, and some

even in the writings of St. Paul (such as Titus iii. 10 ;
1 Cor. v. 11) lend countenance to such a course of
life ; to say nothing of the examples of men who were
specially called to live apart from the world, such as
Elijah, Elisha, and the Holy Baptist. But there are,
undoubtedly, other men and women who possess the
rare gift of being in the world, and yet not of the
world, who can really imitate that part of the conduct
of the Apostle of the Gentiles, wherein he describes
himself (1 Cor. ix. 19–23) as becoming all things to
all men in the hope of at least saving some. The
talents and opportunities of Hilary were such as to
fit him for such a line of conduct, and consequently
to justify him in adopting it.

As a layman, Hilary held a position of some kind
not unsuited to his rank and education. He was
either one of the officers attached to the court of the
Governor of Gaul, known as *curiales*, or else a municipal magistrate. There is a great charm and beauty
attendant on the course pursued by many of God's
commissioned servants, who, like a Samuel in the
Mosaic dispensation, or a Timothy in the Christian,
have been trained from their very childhood in such
a way as to prepare them for the duties of the
sanctuary. But it must not be forgotten, that many
of those not so trained have brought with them into
the service of the ministry many useful acquirements
capable of sanctification and most efficient for the
propagation of the faith, and the building up of
Christ's Church,—tact, knowledge of the world,
habits of order, authority, and perception of the
best ways of influencing for their good the men

and women around them. The knowledge of Greek
literature as well of a holier lore, and the possession
of the rights of Roman citizenship, contributed not a
little to the efficiency of that most illustrious propa-
gator of truth, once known as the persecutor, Saul
of Tarsus. The annals of the early Church furnish
a long list of martyrs, of apologists, of missionaries,
of bishops, and confessors, who came forth (to adopt
an image of St. Augustine's) out of Egypt, laden
with its spoils ; who brought to their new duties their
knowledge of philosophy, of rhetoric, or of human law
and government. Hilary of Poitiers has no claim
to a place among those trained from infancy to be
teachers for priests and rulers of the Church; but
he has a claim to a high and honoured position in
the catalogue of those who, having been originally
among the children of this world, have, by God's
grace, won their way into the ranks of the children
of light.

That which happened to St. Ambrose and to some
other distinguished converts to Christianity during
the first four centuries fell also to the lot of Hilary.
From being merely a layman, he was invited by his
friends and fellow-citizens to become the bishop of
his native town. That such suddenness of elevation
would, in most cases, prove perilous, both to the
person so advanced and to the diocese intrusted to
his charge, can hardly be doubted. But there are
exceptions to all rules, and the case of Hilary is one
of them. He thoroughly justified the choice.

CHAPTER IV.

FIRST YEARS OF HILARY'S EPISCOPATE.

THE predecessor of Hilary in the see of Poitiers died in A.D. 353. It is believed, that his name was Maxentius, and that he was brother to another prelate of great piety, afterwards known as St. Maximin of Trèves. The commencement of Hilary's episcopate dates from the same year (353). He had not courted this promotion; but the objections arising from his humility had been over-ruled. In addition to the usual duties of the episcopal office, two subjects engaged the especial notice of the new bishop. Of these, one was the want of a continuous commentary on some book of the New Testament; the other, the contest against Arianism.

At this period Christians, who understood Latin only, and not Greek—and this was the condition of the great majority of Christians in Gaul and through-out the Western Church generally—did not possess any commentary on an Epistle or Gospel. They could read, indeed, forcible apologies for the faith against heathenism, and many excellent tractates upon various Christian duties; but they had no complete explanation of any single book of the New Testament.

It is justly reckoned among the most eminent

claims of Hilary to our regard, that he was the first among the divines of the West who perceived this want, and attempted to supply it. He published a commentary in Latin on the Gospel of St. Matthew. It must be remembered, that what we now call the modern languages could hardly yet be said to exist for any literary purposes. Latin in the western part of the Roman Empire, and Greek in the eastern, were the two languages known respectively to the largest number of people. For an account of this work, as also Hilary's comments upon the Psalms, we must refer the reader to a later chapter. It must be enough·to say, for the present, that Hilary by this act laid not only Gaul, but all the Latin-speaking Christian communities, under an obligation. Brought to knowledge of the truth by study of the Scriptures, he was anxious to help others to a rightful under-standing of their meaning.

The contest of Hilary against Arianism must also form the subject of a separate consideration. But a few words must be said in this place respecting the position of the Arians in Gaul.

The see which of all others took the leading place in this province, that of Arelas (now known as Arles), was unfortunately at this period occupied by a vehe-ment Arian. His name was Saturninus, and he is conspicuous as being the chief opponent, throughout the whole period before us, of the Bishop of Poitiers, the chief defender of the orthodox faith in Gaul. Hilary shows, as a rule, so much consideration for opponents, that we are bound to believe that he is not speaking without warrant, when he describes this

or that adversary as exceptionally violent and un-
scrupulous.   Another writer, Sulpicius Severus, quite
agrees with Hilary in his accounts of Saturninus.   He
was assisted by two other prelates, named respectively
Ursacius and Valens.   Their reputation is somewhat
fairer than that of Saturninus.   But their course of
action, if less violent than his, was decidedly more
inconsistent and uncertain.   So completely had, by
this time, the great name of Athanasius become
associated with the defence of the faith, that the
attacks or support of the truths enshrined in the
Nicene Creed were frequently combined with the
condemnation or the acquittal of the famous Bishop
of Alexandria.   Now, Ursacius and Valens, at a
council held at Milan in A.D. 355, first voted for the
acquittal of Athanasius, but subsequently changed
their minds, and supported a vote for his condemnation.   There are moments when the treatment of a
man affects the public mind far more keenly than
the discussion of a doctrine.   This changefulness on
the part of these two bishops seems to have alienated
many from their cause.   A clear majority of the
bishops of Gaul separated themselves from the communion of Ursacius, Valens, and Saturninus, and
recognised Hilary as their leader in the work of
"earnestly contending for the faith once for all
delivered to the saints."[1]

It may well be asked, How did Hilary arrive so
soon at a position of such prominence?   The see

[1] Epistle of Jude, iii.   The word rendered *once* in the Authorised Version may fairly be understood as implying *once for
all*.   It is thus translated in the Revised Version.

of Poitiers was not a leading one, such as that of
Arles, nor so famous as many others in Gaul, as, for
example, those of Lyons or Vienne. He had been
little more than two years a bishop, and had by no
means courted eminence. All that can be said is,
that Hilary seems to have carried with him a natural
weight of influence. That his social position, his
good education (so much above that of the majority),
his knowledge of the world, all contributed to this
result, is highly probable. But these gifts would not
have sufficed, had not his brother-bishops been convinced that they had found in him a defender of the
faith at once resolute, able, and charitable. They
waived the considerations of the position of the see
of Poitiers, and the short tenure of the episcopate
by its bishop. Justly, it would seem, has a famous
German writer of this century[1] applied to Hilary
the remark which Gibbon has made with reference
to his contemporary, Athanasius, that " in a time
of public danger the dull claims of age and rank are
sometimes superseded."

[1] Möhler, "Athanasius der Grosse," book v.

CHAPTER V.

HILARY IN EXILE.

THE power of sending obnoxious persons into banishment was one of the most terrible possessed by the
Roman emperors. In the case of an accusation
involving the risk of capital punishment, we know
that "it was not the manner of the Romans to deliver any man to die before that he which was accused
had the accusers face to face, and had licence to
answer for himself concerning the charge laid against
him" (Acts xxv. 16). But in the case of exile no
such fairness was maintained. Augustus sent into
banishment, far from Rome, into the frozen regions
of the banks of the Danube near the Black Sea, the
celebrated poet, Ovid; and to this day no one knows
what was the real cause of the sentence passed upon
him. Utterly different from the lax and too often
immoral pagan poet as was the pure and high-souled
Christian prelate, there is this much in common
between the two cases, that we are ignorant in both
of them of the real grounds of the imperial wrath.
Augustus did, indeed, specify a charge—namely, the
bad tone of Ovid's poetry; but that this was the real
ground of offence has not found credence with a
single historian, ancient or modern. Constantius,
the emperor, who made Hilary an exile, never vouch-

safed to explain the precise charge on which the
sentence was based. From private sources, Hilary
found reason to think that Saturninus of Arles, who
had won the ear of Constantius, had persuaded the
emperor, not merely that the Bishop of Poitiers was
a dangerous and turbulent person, in a political point
of view, but that he had been guilty of some crime
which was morally disgraceful.

The sentence was passed upon Hilary in A.D. 356,
shortly after a council of bishops had been held at
Beziers (then called *Biterra*), in the province subsequently known as Languedoc. Saturninus probably
presided at this meeting. Hilary, with some orthodox
bishops, was present ; but he declares that he was
refused a hearing. In fact, as at many other provincial councils held at this period, the Arians were
clearly in a majority.

During the previous year, Hilary had received a
visit from one who was, like himself, a convert
to the Christian faith. The name of the visitor
was Martin. He is generally regarded as a pupil of
Hilary; and it is very possible that Hilary, who was
by far the more highly educated, even if not the
senior, may have been able to do much for Martin
in the way of instruction. But this learner was
already making himself a name by his zeal and
eloquence, and his visit was looked upon as a
fresh testimony to the fervour and the orthodoxy of
Hilary. In after-times, Hilary's friend was destined
to be known as St. Martin of Tours, and to become,
of all saints, the most popular in the traditions of
his native land. Nor was this favourable estimate

confined to Gaul; it crossed the Channel, and spread
in Britain. To this day, one of our oldest ecclesiastical buildings is known as the church of St.
Martin, in Canterbury. The strength thus lent to
Hilary was further increased by the changeful conduct of the Arians, Ursacius and Valens, to which
reference has already been made. Many who had
been inclined to Arianism were repelled by this
wavering line of procedure, and had rallied around
Hilary. But it pleased God's providence that his
leadership in Gaul should, as we have seen, be rudely
interrupted.

Hilary was ordered by Constantius to betake
himself to the province of Phrygia, in Asia Minor.
Rarely, indeed, was any attempt made to disobey an
imperial mandate of this nature. Hilary, like most
victims of such orders, went straight to the province
pointed out to him, and remained in Phrygia for
somewhat more than three years,—from the summer
of 356 to the autumn of 359.

The Bishop of Poitiers was one of those persons
to whom idleness is insupportable. He contrived to
send orders, from time to time, to the clergy of his
diocese. They were thoroughly loyal to him; and
his wishes, when known, were as completely carried
out in his absence as when he was in the midst of his
flock. Not being, by the terms of his sentence, absolutely confined to one spot, Hilary took advantage of
the liberty allowed him to examine into the state of
religion in such parts of Asia Minor as he could
reach. His impressions were exceedingly unfavour-
able; and he has not left us a good report of his

brother-bishops in that province. Part of the evil
prevalent arose from misunderstandings. On the
one hand, the bishops in Gaul imagined that their
brethren in Asia were right-down Arians. This was
a mistake. They were mostly semi-Arians. The
Asiatic prelates fancied, on the other hand, that the
bishops of Gaul were lapsing into the error known
as Sabellianism. The consideration of these errors
must form the subject of a separate chapter. For
the present, it is enough to say that Hilary took great
pains to remove these mutual misapprehensions, and
that his efforts were attended, though not immediately,
with a very considerable measure of success.

Meanwhile, some more local councils were held,
two at Sirmium (now called Szerem), in Sclavonia,
and one at Ancyra, in Galatia. We may suppose
from the tone of these gatherings, as compared with
others of the three years previous, the current of
opinion among Christians was undergoing some
change. For whereas, between the years 353–356
inclusive, councils held at Arles, at Milan, and at
Beziers, had all proved Arian, two of those named
above had been semi-Arian, which was an improvement; and one, the first of Sirmium, could almost
claim to have been orthodox in character. It is,
however, possible that these differences depended
upon circumstances connected with place rather than
with time.

But neither communications with friends in Gaul,
nor interviews with Christians in Phrygia, nor attention to the affairs of these councils, could suffice to
fill up all the leisure time of a bishop who had now

no diocese to administer, except indirectly, nor ordi-
nations nor confirmations to hold, nor, it would seem,
any sermons to deliver.

The consequence was, that Hilary undertook the
composition of two very important treatises, of which
we must say more hereafter—his books on Synods
("De Synodis"), and that upon the Holy Trinity
("De Trinitate"). The former, which is chiefly historical, is an olive-branch stretched out to the semi-
Arians—one of those conciliatory treatises which, in
modern times, is known as an *Irenicon*. The latter,
a much larger and more important composition, is to
a large extent positive in its teaching; but several of
its books are occupied with answering objections, and
those objections are almost exclusively Arian ones.

CHAPTER VI.

THE QUESTIONS AT ISSUE.

BEFORE any one can convince himself that it is his duty to encounter danger, and possibly death, for the sake of a particular doctrine, he must needs satisfy his own heart and conscience on two questions. The first is, whether the religion for which he meditates a combat is worth preserving; the second, whether the doctrine which is assailed is an essential part of that religion.

On the question, Whether Christianity is worth preserving, we possess, in our day, a mass of evidence which in earlier ages did not exist. Many thinkers, who do not commit themselves to the acceptance of the Christian faith, acknowledge the wonderful amount of good which it has effected for the human race. Even Gibbon, at the commencement of the chapters intended to undermine its influence, admits that it is the religion professed by "the most distinguished portion of human kind in arts and learning, as well as in arms." The beauty of the character of its Founder has been recognised by unbelievers, such as Rousseau and J. S. Mill. Its extraordinary influence in the correction of social vices has been portrayed with much fulness, and with the most earnest desire

to be fair, by Mr. Lecky.[1] This learned and gifted
writer, while stating all that seems to him most faulty
or deficient in Christian tenets and practices, maintains that Christianity revolutionised public opinion
in regard to the sanctity of human life, the universality
of human brotherhood, the value of purity. In the
age of Hilary, Christianity had not had time to leaven
society, and much of the argument in its favour
was consequently inaccessible. One thing, however,
Christians had, which we rarely possess, in the way
of demonstration of their superiority. They had
besides them the actual working of paganism. A
Christian writer of our own time[2] has declared that
it is almost necessary to have lived in non-Christian
lands in order to appreciate the work of Christianity.
In the Europe of the fourth century the manners,
the rites, the morals of paganism were still a living
reality. It is not necessary to exaggerate those evils,
or to forget how painfully short of its own ideal
Christian life has constantly fallen. But the contrast,
nevertheless, is great and deep. Hilary could have
no hesitation in answering the question whether, even
on grounds short of the highest, Christianity was
worth preserving.

The second question may possibly present, or, at
least, seem to present, greater difficulties. It is not
to be denied that, from time to time, some assault of
controversy has been thought likely to endanger the
very citadel of Christianity, which, on further investi-

<hr>

[1] " History of European Morals from Augustus to Charle-
magne." London, 1877, 3rd edit.
[2] Sir Charles Trevelyan in " Long Vacation Studies."

gation, has been proved to be a mere attack upon an
outwork, and an outwork, moreover, of which the
retention is of little importance.   Even so great a
man as St. Augustine imagined that to admit the
existence of people living at the antipodes would
imperil the Christian faith.   How far the Copernican
system of astronomy lies under condemnation among
our Roman Catholic fellow-Christians may be a moot
point.   That when taught by Galileo it caused profound alarm, and that he was in some measure persecuted for his proclamation of it, is unquestionable.
Again, many learned and excellent persons in our
own day have regarded as a vital question, the precise
theory adopted by us respecting the mode in which
the sacrifice of our Lord's death wrought the redemption of the human race.   Others, again, have used
language which would almost seem to imply that the
entire fabric of Christian doctrine would collapse, if
the commonly-accepted date or authorship of a single
book of the Bible were found to be incorrect.

There are not wanting those, especially among
sceptics and bystanders, who maintain that the
solemn truth, of which Hilary in the West and
Athanasius in the East were the most conspicuous
champions, is a question of this nature.   This is not
the place for an elaborate refutation of a grave and
deadly error; but it must be observed, that the
opposite conviction, namely, that the divinity of our
Lord is the central truth of our holy faith, is the conviction of the overwhelming majority of those who profess and call themselves Christians.   So completely
is this the case where definitions in accordance with

it have been given, that it would be almost impossible to detect from internal evidence to what denomination of Christians the writer belonged. "The Christian religion," writes one, " that is to say, the redemption of men by a God made man." Or, again, in the fuller statement of another, "What is, in fact, Christianity? what is its fundamental position, the base, the substance of all its doctrines? What is the Gospel, that is to say, the news which it announces to the world? It is that, in consequence of an original and hereditary enfeeblement, man—every man without distinction—had lost the power of fulfilling, and even of knowing his duty, and would, consequently, perish without a chance of safety if God had not come in human form to reopen to him the sources of virtue, of pardon, and of life. Therein lies the sum of Christianity. It is only Christians who sign that creed." In like manner, a poet of this age in speaking of another poet, Robert Browning, describes him as one who "holds with a force of personal passion the radical tenet of the Christian faith—faith in Christ as God—a tough, hard, vital faith, that can bear at need hard stress of weather and hard thought."

Once more. "The essence of the belief is the belief in the divinity of Christ. Every view of history, every theory of our duty, must be radically transformed by contact with that stupendous mystery. Unsectarian Christianity consists in shirking the difficulty without meeting it, and trying hard to believe that the passion can survive without its essential basis. It proclaims the love of Christ as our motive,

whilst it declines to make up its mind whether Christ
was God or man; or endeavours to escape a cate-
gorical answer under a cloud of unsubstantial rhetoric.
But the difference between God and man is infinite,
and no effusion of superlatives will disguise the plain
fact from honest minds.   To be a Christian in any
real sense, you must start from a dogma of the most
tremendous kind, and an undogmatic creed is as
senseless as a statue without shape, or a picture
without colour."   Of the authors of these words, two
are Christians; but the last two quotations are taken
from writings of avowed unbelievers in Christianity.

The position of dogmas in the scheme of Christian
doctrine has been not inaptly likened to that of the
bones in the animal frame.   Of course, such a comparison must needs remind us that the skeleton is not
the man; veins and arteries, nerves and muscles,
organs of the senses, flesh and skin, and much
besides, are needed for the completeness of the
structure into which its Maker breathed a soul.
But certainly the boneless creatures, such as the
jelly-fish, occupy a low place in the scale of creation,
and a religion without dogmas would resemble them.
To dwell on dogma only would result in an equally
imperfect sort of religion.   Such a religion would be
cold and dry.

It must also be conceded that from time to time
there has been manifested in almost every Christian
community a tendency to erect into a dogma some
tenet which, at the best, can only be regarded as a
pious opinion.   This is a real infringement upon
Christian liberty, and it inevitably does harm in many

ways, more especially by throwing suspicion on the dogmatic principle. That the border-line may in some cases be difficult to draw is undeniable, but, generally speaking, a dogma may be defined as "a fundamental principle of saving truth, expressed or implied in Holy Scripture, taught by the Church Universal, and consonant to sound reason." It may well be doubted whether any corporate body can be held together without some essential principle or set of principles correspondent to dogma. Certainly it must be difficult to name any religion that has lived and energised, apart from the dogmatic principle. In a drama of the last century, " Nathan the Wise," its author, the celebrated Lessing, appears to suggest that the good specimens of the Mahometan, the Jewish, and the Christian religion therein portrayed prove the unimportance of dogma. It is somewhat singular that he should have drawn representatives of the three most dogmatic religions in the world, the Jewish, the Mahometan, and the Christian. All three repose upon the basis of belief in the unity of the living God, a future life, and judgment to come.

We may seem to have wandered very far from the fourth century and the city of Poitiers, and the eminent bishop of whose life and times we are treating ; but we are convinced that a realisation of the continued prominence and importance of certain questions in our own day must help us in the attempt to appreciate fairly the conduct and character of the men of earlier ages. To throw ourselves back by a vigorous effort of the imagination into times in many

respects, so unlike our own is, indeed, most desirable.
The task, however, though well worth essaying, is not
always easy.   But this much we may all be able to
perceive, that a question which is vital in the nineteenth century may well have been as vital in the
fourth century.   If, indeed, we have made up our
minds that Christianity is not worth preserving, then
martyrs, confessors, reformers of all time have made
a woful mistake, and we cannot possibly sympathise
with them, far less feel gratitude to their memories.
In like manner, if we can persuade ourselves that it
is unimportant whether our Lord be simply a creature,
or God Incarnate, then, of course, those who underwent persecution on behalf of His Godhead must
be regarded as foolish men, who contended for a
shadow.

But we are writing specially for those who believe
in the Christian faith, and who accept as among its
most fundamental tenets the doctrine of the Incarnation, as well as that of the Holy Trinity.   At the
risk of some seeming repetition, it will be necessary
to set down here the Catholic faith on each of these
verities, and the particular deflections from them,
against which Hilary made it the business of his life
to contend.

And, in the first place, as concerns the Holy
Trinity.   The following are among the leading propositions concerning the Great Being whose creatures
we are.   God is One.   He has existed from all
eternity.   Nothing can have come into being without His good-will and pleasure.   Consequently, those
who imagined that matter is eternal—a common

mistake among the heathen—were, though perhaps not always intentionally, denying God's Almightiness ; for, if anything has existed without His good-will and pleasure, it is evident that He is not Almighty. There was, then, a long eternity, when as yet created things were not, and God reigned alone—alone, but not solitary, for that in the Oneness of the Godhead there was ever inter-communion between the three Persons, Father, Son, and Holy Ghost. "Before the mountains were brought forth, or ever Thou hadst formed the earth and the world, even from everlasting to everlasting, Thou art God." But there never was a time when the eternal Father had not with Him His image,[1] the eternal Son ; just as—if such poor earthly illustrations may be pardoned—a twig growing by the water-side has from the first its own reflected image ever by it. There never was a time when there did not proceed, from the Father immediately, from the Son mediately, the Holy Ghost. The Father is the One God, the Son is the One God, the Holy Ghost is the One God ; and yet the Father is not the Son, nor the Son the Holy Ghost, nor the Holy Ghost the Father. Further, though all three Persons are of one substance, power, majesty, and eternity, yet is a certain priority of dignity conceived to reside in the Father, forasmuch as He is represented in Holy Scripture as being ministered to by the Son and the Spirit, but never as ministering ; as

---

[1] Illustrations must not be pressed. St. Augustine, from whom this is adopted, is careful to point out that it only exemplifies an equality of time, not one of nature like the oneness of the Father and the Son.

sending, but never sent; as begotten of none, proceeding from none, being the source and origin of Godhead.

What are the mistakes on this lofty theme to which even devout and believing minds are liable? They are two. It is possible to dwell so much upon the separate work of each Person as virtually to make three Gods. This is the error known as Tritheism. A tendency in this direction is probably exhibited by persons who allow themselves to regard the Son as the more merciful, the Father the more severe; for this at once introduces into the Divine Being a separation of will.

The other error seems to arise from a wish to escape from mystery. And yet it would in reality be an argument against the truth of any representation of the Divine Nature, if it involved an entire freedom from mystery. Even our own finite and created natures have about them a great deal of mystery,—"we are fearfully and wonderfully made." How, then, can we expect that revealed truth concerning the Creator should be devoid of mystery? We cannot, indeed, believe that which is contrary to reason; but we surely may be ready to accept that there is that which is above and beyond reason.

Now, this other error lies in regarding the threefold Personality as being only an exhibition of the same Being, so to speak, in different relations to us. These erroneous teachers spoke of the Triune Godhead in language which, in fact, represented God as One *Person*. They said, according to Epiphanius, that as in one man there is body, soul, and spirit;[1] so the Father resembled the body, the Son the soul, and the Holy Ghost the Spirit. Such was the teaching of a heretic of the second century, named Sabellius ; whence the error itself is commonly termed Sabellianism. As, however, it would involve the unscriptural inference that the Father had suffered on our behalf, it was also sometimes known by a word expressive of this tenet. This other name was Patri-passianism, and its adherents were accordingly sometimes called Patri-passians and sometimes Sabellians. A profound thinker of the Middle Ages, the great schoolman Aquinas, declares that we are all tempted sometimes towards imagining too great a separation, sometimes too great an identification of the Persons of the ever-blessed Trinity, and that thus the human mind, if it be not watchful, may alternately be swayed in the direction of Tritheism and in that of Sabellianism. There is, probably, much truth in this remark, and the caution is one for which we should be grateful.

It would not have been necessary to introduce the subject of Sabellianism into this sketch, but for the fact to which reference has been made—that the bishops of Gaul, who supported Hilary in his struggle against Arianism, were suspected of that error. The suspicion seems to have been a thoroughly erroneous one. It probably arose from a misunderstanding of the Greek term *Homöousion*, which, though it means *of one substance*, or *of one being*, was never intended

---

[1] " II.rereses," cap. 62.

by the Greek-speaking theologians to indicate Oneness of Personality.

But the second great truth of the Gospel Revelation, the Incarnation of our Lord, was the main subject of debate at this time. Christianity brought before the world an idea, an institution, and a Person. The idea, if we may attempt to grasp the leading idea of a religion so profound and far-reaching, may, perhaps, be stated thus,—a blending of the human with the divine, which should be recognised as at once pure and reverent, awful and merciful, subduing and elevating, historical and yet eternal. It is almost needless to observe, that the attempts made to reach such an idea in other religions all fail in some of these particulars. The legends of Greece and Rome are too often the very reverse of pure. The incarnations of Vishnu, narrated in Hindoo records, are neither reverent nor enduring. How completely the historic element is lacking to them may be gathered from one single fact, that we do not know the date, nor anything like the date, of any one of those Sanskrit books which are regarded by Hindoos as sacred.

As an institution, the amount of freedom combined with order exhibited in the Church became an object of admiration to the natives of countries which were either suffering from sheer anarchy, or else weighed down by despotism. Indeed, Gibbon names among the causes of the spread of Christianity the excellence of its organisation ; and, though his ways of solving the problem of its growth are quite inadequate, and in many respects erroneous, yet he is not altogether wrong in his selection; and this is a point which, so far as it reaches, contains at least a measure of truth.

An idea may possess great power. The idea of national independence has played a large part in history; witness the annals of ancient Greece, of Switzerland, of Scotland, or of modern Italy. Institutions may also mould the mind of nations; those attributed to Lycurgus certainly moulded the mind of Sparta. But no idea, nor cycle of ideas, no institution, however well organised, could have won the reverence, the obedience, the enthusiasm, which the Christian religion won by its exhibition of the Person of its Founder. "In addition to all the characters of Hebrew Monotheism, there exists, in the doctrine of the Cross, a peculiar and inexhaustible treasure for the affectionate feelings. The idea of the God-man, the God whose goings forth have been from everlasting, yet visible to men for their redemption as an earthly temporal creature, living, acting, and suffering among themselves; then—which is yet more important—transferring to the unseen place of His spiritual agency the same humanity He wore on earth, so that the lapse of generations can in no way affect the conception of His identity; *this is the most powerful thought that ever addressed itself to a human imagination.* It is the fulcrum which alone was wanting to move the world. Here was solved at once the great problem which so long had distressed the teachers of mankind, how to make virtue the object of passion, and to secure at once the warmest enthusiasm in the heart, with the clearest perception

of right and wrong in the understanding. The character of the Blessed Founder of our faith became an
abstract of morality to determine the judgment, while
at the same time it remained personal and liable to
love. The Written Word and Established Church
prevented a degeneration into ungoverned mysticism,
but the predominant principle of vital religion always
remained that of self-sacrifice to the Saviour. Not
only the higher divisions of moral duties, but the
simple, primary impulse of benevolence, were sub-
ordinated to this new absorbing passion. The world
was loved 'in Christ alone.' The brethren were
members of His mystical body. All the other bonds
that had fastened down the Spirit of the Universe
to our narrow round of earth were as nothing in
comparison to this golden chain of suffering and
self-sacrifice, which at once riveted the heart of man
to One who, like Himself, was acquainted with grief.
Pain is the deepest thing we have in our nature, and
union through pain has always seemed more holy
and more real than any other."[1]

Now, as it pleased God, doubtless for wise ends,
to allow that controversies should arise, it was natural
that those which concerned the Person of the great
Prophet who taught this creed should be among the
first to occupy the attention of Christendom; for
that question, it must be repeated, touches the very
essentials of Christianity. Between those who worship
Christ, as God of God, the second Person of the
adorable Trinity, and those who make Him a creature,

---

[1] "Remains of Arthur Hallam." He died at the age of 22,
and is the subject of the Laureate's " In Memoriam."

there must needs be a great gulf. True, that the latter class may say that He is no ordinary man; that He is the noblest, best, purest, and highest of all creatures. But, on this supposition, He is still a creature; and to give to a creature the honour due to God alone is the very essence of idolatry.

Now this—when veils of subtlety are torn away—this question, and nothing less, had been the subject of discussion at the Council of Nice. The sceptical historian, to·whom reference has just been made, exhibits in his narrative many strange anomalies. Carried away by the grandeur of Athanasius, Gibbon has drawn a picture of that great man, not, indeed, appreciative in the same sense as that given by Hooker, but yet so full of life and vigour, that good judges have pronounced it superior to that contained in the pages of any ecclesiastical historian. Nevertheless, his love of gibes has induced him to suggest, that because the respective watchwords of the orthodox, and of the Arians, or at least the Semi-Arians, differed but in a single letter, the difference between the two was vague, shadowy, and by no means vital.

Whether Gibbon really believed this, whether he could have persuaded himself, that such a man, as he acknowledges Athanasius to be, would have written and argued, toiled and suffered, through his long career for the sake of a mere phantom, a splitting of words, seems very doubtful. But he has contrived to impress the motion, not only upon large masses of ordinary readers, but on the minds of many men of eminence, especially among such as, however great in the domain of scholarship, or physical

science, have never bestowed much real thought
upon questions of theology.

It is true that the terms, " of one substance," and
" of like substance " (ὁμοούσιον, ὁμοιούσιον), do, in
the original language of the Nicene Creed, differ
but by a single letter. It is equally true, that the
word *Creatour*, as it used to be spelt, differs by one
letter only from the word *creature*. Both Arius and
Athanasius knew perfectly well that their respective
watchwords did involve that vital difference. After-
ages have clearly shown this. In our own day we
might search the wide world over, and scarcely
anywhere should we find a congregation of Arians,
still less of Semi-Arians. Their position has been
felt to be untenable. But the position to which the
teaching of Arius was sure to lead, namely, that
Christ is a mere man, is that of hundreds who
acknowledge His historic existence. And still the
truth for which the opponents of Arius contended,
the divinity of our Lord and Saviour, is to the
faithful the life's life of their spiritual being,—

> The holy Church throughout all the world doth acknow-
>   ledge Thee,
> The Father of an infinite majesty ;
> Thine honourable, true, and only Son ;
> Also the Holy Ghost, the Comforter.

Whether, indeed, those who maintain that the
Founder of Christianity, if a mere man, can be
regarded as a good man, is one of the serious difficulties which must be faced by Socinians and their
allies. This has been forcibly pointed out by writers
of our own day, as by Canon Liddon in his "Bampton

Lectures," and by the author of a short treatise especially dedicated to its consideration.[1] We believe that it will become more and more evident, to those who really study the question, that to maintain that Jesus Christ was simply human, and was yet humble and devout, is to defend a position which is logically inconsistent and untenable.

[1] "The Great Dilemma," by the Rev. H. B. Ottley. London: C. Kegan Paul & Co., 1881

CHAPTER VII.

HILARY AND THE ARIANS.

ATHANASIUS stands in the front rank of that great contest to which reference has just been made. It is some satisfaction to find in the present day writers who either look on the matter from outside as calm spectators, or else are actually hostile to Christianity, entirely abjuring the notion that the cause, of which the Bishop of Alexandria was the prime champion, could possibly be one of trivial importance.

But, though Athanasius was the leader, he never found sufficient leisure for the production of any very long or elaborate treatise, and he only addressed those who could understand the Greek language. Here it was that Hilary came so powerfully to the aid of his fellow-labourer in the cause of truth. The act of Constantius, which for more than three years deprived the diocese of Poitiers of Hilary's superintendence, left the bishop at leisure, as has been remarked, for the composition of the twelve books "De Trinitate," of which so many are occupied with a refutation of Arianism. This work was widely read, and it must have proved a mine from which men of less leisure and ability might extract a large mass of valuable material. It supplied all—some would say even more than all—to the readers of

Latin, which was given by Athanasius in his "Orations against the Arians" to the readers of Greek.

It will be seen also, in our next chapter, that all the acts and writings of Hilary which tended to bring back Semi-Arians to the faith, must have, at least indirectly, had the effect of weakening the cause of Arianism. Among the *writings* having this object in view must be named Hilary's treatise, "De Synodis," and a history of the Councils of Seleucia and of Rimini, of which we have only fragments. Among his *actions* in the same direction, we must include his labours in France after his return from Phrygia; and also a visit to Italy.

To Hilary, as to Athanasius, the contest against Arianism seems to have presented itself in that light in which we have already attempted to place it namely, as a practical answer to the questions whether Christianity was worth preserving, and whether the doctrine of the Redeemer's Godhead was an essential element of Christianity? If both these questions were to be answered in the affirmative, then exile, with loss of the charities and comforts of home life; then toil and thought and study; then conferences with supporters and with misguided opponents; then breaches of friendship with the authorities of the state; then even occasional misunderstandings with personal friends must all be worth enduring, in consideration of the example and commands of Christ, of the teaching of His Apostles, and of the greatness of the issue at stake, which embraces not only time, but eternity. " To this end was I born, and for this cause came I into the world

that I should bear witness unto the Truth. . . . .
Though we, or an angel from heaven, preach any
other gospel unto you than that which we have
preached unto you, let him be accursed. . . . . Many
deceivers are come into the world, who confess not
that Jesus Christ is come in the flesh. This is a
deceiver and an anti-Christ. . . . . It was needful for
me to write unto you, and exhort you that ye should
earnestly contend for the faith which was once for all
delivered unto the saints." [1]

We inherit in peace the results of the toils and
sufferings of these confessors of the fourth century.
Is it well for us to criticise with severity any mistakes
which they may have made? to censure lightly any
rare and occasional asperities of language which they
may have employed? or to be wholly careless and
unthankful for the examples which they have set for
their many wise and loving words for the victories
won by them, of which we of later ages reap the
benefits?

[1] St. John xviii. 37; Galatians i. 8; 2 St. John 7; St.
Jude 3.

CHAPTER VIII.

HILARY AND THE SEMI-ARIANS.

WE are all aware that, in contests concerning literature, or art, or politics, it is not uncommon to find
men who are instinctively drawn to take a middle
course. Such men would not in the field of letters
take part wholly with what are known respectively as
the classic or the romantic schools. In art they
would shrink alike from the ardent denunciation of
the Renaissance spirit which the author of "Modern
Painters" and "The Stones of Venice" employs,
and from the vehement reaction which has now set
in upon the other side. In politics, they would,
perhaps, proclaim themselves what we now call
Liberal-Conservatives. Few but extreme enthusiasts
would deny the possible rightfulness of such a position. Indeed, to many minds it comes with a prestige
in its favour, as the exhibition of a judicial temper.

It must, however, be evident that such a principle
carries with it dangers of its own. A famous Greek
philosopher,[1] from finding that, as a matter of fact,
virtues generally lay between two extremes, one of
excess and another of defect, actually taught that this
was part of the essence of virtue, and introduced it

[1] Aristotle, "Nicomachean Ethics," book ii., chap. 6, &c.

into his definition.   But the theory burdens his
scheme of morals with difficulties, which he has not
solved.   Is it, for example, possible for a man to be
really too just ?   Is it conceivable that a heart could
be too pure?   Surely more deep and true is the
enunciation of our Christian philosopher, Bishop
Butler, when he speaks of truth or right being " something real in itself, and so not to be judged of by its
liableness to abuse, or by its supposed distance from,
or nearness to, error."   Most especially must Butler's
remark be applicable to any truth which we believe
that God Himself has revealed to us.

Semi-Arianism looks like one of these attempts to
take a middle course, where no middle course was in
reality possible.   Viewed as a system of theology,
Semi-Arianism is as untenable as Arianism.   It involved, as has truly been said, the following contradictions : " That the Son was born before all times,
yet not eternal ; not a creature, yet not God ; of His
substance, yet not the same in substance ; and His
perfect and exact resemblance in all things, yet not a
second Deity."[1]   An English theologian of the last
century, Dr. Clarke, who seems to have been almost
a Semi-Arian, was asked whether upon his theory
he supposed that God the Father could annihilate the
Son and the Holy Ghost.[2]   After long consideration,
he avowed himself unable to reply.   Of course, he

---

[1] " The Arians of the Fourth Century," by J. H. Newman,
chap. iv. sec. ii.

[2] This debate is referred to by Canon Liddon, and authorities given in his Bampton Lectures, sec. i., note *t.*   The
writer knew it traditionally from boyhood.

perceived that an answer either in the affirmative or in the negative would be equally fatal to his theory. If the Father could annihilate the Son and the Spirit, then they must be merely creatures. If he could not annihilate them, this could only be because they are one with Himself, of equal power, majesty, and glory.

Now, it might naturally be supposed from these considerations that the champions of the Nicene Faith would practically regard Semi-Arians in the same light as that in which they regarded Arians ; and, indeed, there was one school of orthodox thinkers who did so regard them ; who considered the differences between the two sets of opponents too slight to deserve consideration, and who made an absolute admission of the Creed of Nicæa a primary condition of intercommunion and peace. The leader of this section of the orthodox was Lucifer, bishop of Cagliari, or, as he is sometimes called, bishop of Sardinia, the island of which Cagliari is the capital. He was a brave and earnest defender of the faith, but not always wise or considerate.

But on this, as on almost every point of the controversy, Athanasius and Hilary, though separated and in different lands, thought and acted in almost perfect harmony and unison. They both perceived that, though as a theory Semi-Arianism had little if any claim to be thought superior to Arianism, yet that many of the Semi-Arians were in tone and temper of mind exceedingly different from the Arians. There was certainly a detachment of them who appear to have been reverent and unworldly, and who showed keenness in detecting and in repressing other errors of the day. Athanasius, in a well-known passage, declares that those who accepted all that was passed at Nice except the term of one substance (*homöousion*) were to be treated as brothers, whose difference was one of terms rather than of real meaning. He felt confidence that in time they would come to see its value and accept it.

This feeling pervades the treatise on Synods ("De Synodis"), a letter which Hilary, while still in exile, addressed to his brother-bishops in Gaul. They were probably disappointed to find that many of those who had supported the cause of truth at Nice had not shown wisdom or firmness when they returned to their sees; and they desired some explanation of the numerous professions of faith which the Orientals seemed to be putting forth. Their questions had ,a practical bearing, for the Emperor Constantius had ordered that two fresh councils should be held—one for the East, and one for the West of Christendom. The Western one was to meet at Ariminum, on the eastern coast of Italy, the place since known as Rimini,—

> Where Po descends,
> With all his followers, in search of peace.[1]

The place of the Eastern gathering was at first fixed at Nicomedia; but on August the 24th, in A.D. 358, a terrible earthquake all but overthrew the entire

[1]
> Dove il Po descende,
> Per aver pace, co' seguaci sui.
>   DANTE, "Inferno," canto v.,
at the commencement of the sad and well-known story of *Francesca da Rimini*.

city. At the time when Hilary wrote, Ancyra had in consequence been fixed upon, but ultimately Seleucia was chosen.

Now, Hilary was very anxious that his Gallic brethren, and also the British bishops, should come to Rimini in a charitable frame of mind towards the Semi-Arians. He praises his friends in Gaul in his " De Synodis " for their firmness in opposing the Arian bishop of Arles, Saturninus, and considers that they had done well in rejecting some unsatisfactory forms of expression put forth at a recent assembly held at Sirmium. But as regards the Semi-Arian watchword "of *like* substance" (*homoiousion*) he would not have them reject it too hastily without examination. There were those who, from malice or ignorance, had misunderstood the orthodox term " of *one* substance" (*homöousion*) in such wise as to make it identify the Personality of the Son with that of the Father, and become, in fact, a symbol of Sabellianism. Now, as on the one hand the orthodox term might be perverted, so, on the other, was the unorthodox one capable of a good interpretation. Some of those who used it had been frightened from the use of the true word by the misinterpretation, and, when they said " of like substance," did in reality mean to imply an identity of substance, as well as of power, majesty, and glory between the Father and the Son. Asia Minor in general is, writes Hilary, in a sad condition. " I do not speak of things strange; I do not write without knowledge; I have heard and seen in my own person the faults, not of laymen merely, but of bishops ; for excepting Eleusius, and a few with

him, the ten provinces of Asia in which I am, are, for
the most part, truly ignorant of God." Now this
Eleusius, bishop of Cyzicus, was one of the Semi-
Arians. With him Hilary also names, as distinguished
for blamelessness of life, the bishops of Sebaste and
of Ancyra, by name respectively Eustathius and
Basil. The last-named was a man. of high culture
and learning.[1]

From the champions of the Catholic faith in Gaul,
Hilary turns to his friends among the Semi-Arians.
He seems willing to concede the possibility of a creed
being accepted which should embrace both terms ;
or ·that the Son should be described as " being of
one and of like substance with the Father." This
would show that the orthodox did not mean to teach
Sabellianism ; it would also show that the difference
between Arians and Semi-Arians was a vital one,
while that between the Semi-Arians and Catholics
was rather metaphysical and verbal, than in reality
doctrinal. "Grant me," says Hilary to the Semi-
Arians, "that indulgence which I have so often demanded at your hands. *You are not Arians ;* why
do you get the reputation of being Arians by your
denial of the homöousion ?" For his own part, Hilary
had learned his faith from the New Testament, especially the Gospels. "Although I was baptised "—
such are his words—" many years ago, and have held
for some time the office of a bishop, I never heard
the Nicene Creed, until just before the date of my

---

[1] He must not, of course, be confounded with his more celebrated contemporary and namesake, St. Basil, the eloquent and
orthodox bishop of Cæsarea.

exile. But the Gospels and the Apostles made me understand the true sense of the *homöousion* and *homoiousion*. My desires are pious ones. Let us not condemn the Fathers, let us not stir up the heretics, lest, in our attempt to banish heresy, we in reality cherish it."

Such was Hilary's endeavour to act as a peacemaker. It is frequently the fate of such to be suspected, sometimes upon one side, sometimes upon both sides. In the case before us, though the Semi-Arians were not prepared to act upon Hilary's suggestions, they did not, so far as we know, complain of any misrepresentation of their views, nor question the good faith of the writer. But Hilary was not so fortunate on the other side. He ought, one would think, to have been considered above suspicion. His communications with the Emperor Constantius, which we must consider in another chapter, the tone of his commentary on the Gospel of St. Matthew, the very fact that he was now suffering exile as a confessor on behalf of the faith, should have preserved him from assault on the side of the orthodox. But there was an extreme wing, more Athanasian than Athanasius himself—if the expression may be pardoned—who were for rejecting the very semblance of compromise, and thought that the proposals of Hilary had conceded too much to the Semi-Arians. The leader of this set was, as has been intimated, sincere and earnest, but somewhat harsh-minded, Lucifer of Cagliari. It must be owned that there were many Semi-Arians, who were unlike the three " very holy men " (*sanctissimi viri*) to whom Hilary refers ; men to whose shiftings and whose want, either of clearness of understanding, or of straightforwardness of purpose, must have afforded some excuse to the Sardinian prelate. Of Hilary's personal behaviour towards him Lucifer could not, however, have found any reason to complain. For Hilary, as soon as he heard of Lucifer's objection to the "De Synodis," sent Lucifer a copy of the treatise, with an appendage of notes of an apologetic character, concluded in a tone of thorough courtesy and gentleness.

One feature of Semi-Arian reasoning will fall naturally into our next chapter, because it was specially insisted on by the Emperor Constantius. But it will make our narrative clearer if we relate in this place the remainder of Hilary's dealings with the Semi-Arians, although it may carry us a little beyond that period of his exile with which these chapters are specially concerned.

In the autumn of A.D. 359 the two councils summoned by Constantius actually met; the gathering of the Orientals being at Seleucia in Isauria, that of the Occidentals at Rimini. If the better-disposed among the Semi-Arians could have held their own at these two councils, it is probable that the recommendations of Hilary would have been virtually accepted, and comparative tranquillity have been restored. Possibly, however, after all it might have proved a hollow peace; and, if so, the disaster that ensued may have been over-ruled by God's providence to lasting good. That disaster was simply this, that both at Seleucia and at Rimini the Semi-Arians were quite out-manœuvred, though not precisely in the same manner, by the bolder and less scrupulous Arians. As a dweller, though a constrained one, in the East, as the bishop of an important see in the West, Hilary found his career inseparably blended with the acts of both these councils.

At that of Seleucia he was for a time personally present, having been, in fact, compelled to attend it by the secular authorities. There, amidst a gathering of about 150 bishops, Hilary found a comparatively small section of the supporters of orthodoxy, chiefly from Egypt; a considerable number of Semi-Arians, and a party of Ultra-Arians, who, from their watchword of actual unlikeness (*anomœon*) between the Father and the Son, are known in history as the Anomœans. The language of this school so utterly shocked Hilary that he retired from the assembly. He had, indeed, effected some good by taking the opportunity of explaining the true position of his friends in Gaul. It may have also been partially owing to his influence that the leader of the Ultra-Arians, Acacius, found himself unable to carry out his own plans, though he contrived to win so much support from the Semi-Arians as to frustrate any decision in favour of the Creed of Nicæa.

In the Latin council held at Rimini the orthodox bishops were proportionally far more numerous, being no less than 320 out of 400. The imperial commissioners sent by Constantius found that their friends were so outnumbered, that the Nicene Creed would be almost certainly reaffirmed and Arianism again condemned. The council deposed these commissioners, and sent a deputation to Constantinople

to inform the emperor of the sentiment pervading it.
By delays, on the pretext that the barbarian war
demanded his attention, and by threats, Constantius
overawed this deputation.   Valens, the Gallic bishop
already mentioned in an earlier chapter, declared that
he and his friends condemned Arius and Arianism,
and all the well-known watchwords of the sect, such
as the assertions that "there was a time when the
Word was not "; that ." he was a creature as other
creatures "; and the like.   But they entreated the
defenders of the Catholic faith that, for peace sake,
they would give up the term " of one substance "
(*homöousion*), and adopt instead the assertion " that
the Son was *like* the Father" (*homoion*). The majority
gave way, and Valens exulted in his triumph.   The
condemnation of the error " that the Son was not a
creature as other creatures " necessarily left room for
the inference that, after all, not merely as man, but
even before His Incarnation, He was, *in some sense*,
a creature.   And the result of the Council of Rimini
was made famous by the often-quoted words of St.
Jerome, " that the world awoke one morning and
groaned in its astonishment at finding itself Arian."

It will, however, be seen that Hilary, after his
return to Gaul, was not willing to refuse communion,
as many of his allies desired, to all the bishops who
had been led to sign the *formula* adopted at Rimini.
In Italy, where he travelled for a time and spent more
than two years of his later life (A.D. 362–364), this
conciliatory course was attended with partial, but only
partial, success.   But in his native land, where he had
pursued it before the journey to Italy, it proved

thoroughly efficacious. It detached the Semi-Arians from the Arians, and won them back to the truth. It led to the condemnation of Saturninus of Arles, and to the triumph of the Catholic faith on the Holy Trinity and the Incarnation throughout all the Christian parts of Gaul. The friend and pupil of Hilary, Martin of Tours, found, indeed, plenty to do in the way of conversion of his countrymen from heathenism in portions of the land yet unconverted; and a later generation had its own difficulties in southern France, in connexion with the difficult problems respecting grace and free-will, Pelagianism and Semi-Pelagianism. But for the overthrow in Gaul, and beyond its limits, of the first grievous error concerning the adorable Person of the Redeemer of the world, our gratitude is chiefly due to the combination of firmness with charity which marked the life and labours of Hilary.

If, then, we may venture briefly to sum up his sentiments towards the Semi-Arians, they would be found, if we mistake not, to run somewhat as follows :— " There is heresy, and there is heretical pravity. Heresy, or the denial of saving truth, may be uttered by many who are sound at heart, but who have been misled by want of intelligence and of perception of the points really at issue. But heretical pravity means something much worse than this; it is the enunciation of heresy in a really heretical temper of mind, and it can be detected by its tone of irreve rence and its utter unscrupulousness with regard to means. Arius, with his appeals to the unworthy analogies of earthly generation, with the songs for

drinking parties, which embodied his errors, with his
supple courtliness and inveiglement of the civil power
into his schemes, is the very type and embodiment of
heretical pravity.   But the Semi-Arians, though their
creed may be hardly less erroneous, are in many cases
far better than their creed.   They have been often
weak, often dull of perception, and unskilful in the
use of terms, but I have found them often to be reverent towards Holy Scripture, learned, and blameless
of life.   Hence, what may seem at first an inconsistency, my uncompromising attitude towards the
defenders of Arianism ; my moderation towards the
Semi-Arians.   I have taken the men as I found them.
For justification I may in this case, at least, appeal to
the results.   The judgment on my career I leave to
the justice of posterity and the mercy of Him whom
I have tried to serve."

CHAPTER IX.

HILARY AND THE EMPEROR.

THE title which is prefixed to this chapter is open to
a technical objection. A critic might urge against it
that Hilary came into contact with two actual emperors, and with another magnate who became an
emperor during Hilary's lifetime, though at the
epoch when they met he was only recognised as an
heir to the throne; as a Cæsar, not as an Augustus.
The two actual emperors were Constantius II. and
Valentinian; the Cæsar was the youth who was afterwards to be known to all time by the title of Julian
the Apostate.

But the relations of the Bishop of Poitiers with
Julian and with Valentinian, more especially with
the former, were comparatively brief. Waiving once
again, for the sake of convenience, chronological
considerations, we may just state the nature of
these relations, and then put them entirely on one
side.

It will be seen presently that Hilary was suspected
by Constantius of some interference of a hostile
character in matters political. It is rather startling
to find in Hilary's second letter, addressed to that
emperor (about A.D. 360, during his exile), the following language :—" I am an exile, not as the victim

F

of crime, but as that of a faction. I have a weighty witness on behalf of the justice of my complaint, my lord, your religious Cæsar, Julian."

It is a singular circumstance, that although part of the episcopate of Hilary coincided with the short reign of Julian (A.D. 361–363), so that the open apostasy of the dissimulating prince must have become known even in Gaul, we do not hear of any collision between these old acquaintances. It is possible that the intolerant edicts of Julian, which prohibited the Christians from teaching the arts of grammar and of rhetoric, may have hardly had time to operate in Gaul before the death of their author made them null and void; or that Julian may have been too busy with Hilary's great fellow-labourer, Athanasius, to turn his theological attention from the East. "Julian, who despised the Christians, honoured Athanasius with his sincere and peculiar hatred."[1] From his own point of view Julian's sentiments were perfectly natural. He was thoroughly convinced that, if he could crush the primate of Egypt, he would have comparatively little difficulty in overthrowing other rulers of the Church. Athanasius has received many marks of homage, from the days of St. Gregory of Nyssa to those of Hooker;[2] but none, perhaps, more emphatic and complete than the bitter hostility of Julian. The emperor's conduct in this respect was a real illustration of the well-known

[1] Gibbon, "Decline and Fall," chap. xxiii.
[2] "Ecclesiastical Polity," book .v., chap. xlii., sec. 2. Probably the best and finest summary of the career of Athanasius extant in any language.

dictum of a writer of this century, that "nothing is more infallible than the instinct of impiety."

But we must return to Hilary. Besides the brief and apparently favourable intercourse with Julian in Gaul, at the commencement of his episcopate, the Bishop of Poitiers was brought into contact on one occasion with the Emperor Valentinian. This emperor being at Milan in the year A.D. 364, the year of his accession, found Hilary at Milan engaged in a controversy with the bishop of that see, Auxentius.

Hilary was convinced, and apparently with good reason, that Auxentius was in reality an Arian at heart. As, however, the Bishop of Milan made an open profession of the faith proclaimed in the Nicene Creed, we can hardly wonder that Valentinian, viewing the matter as a politician, declined to listen to the evidence that could be adduced against the sincerity of this avowal. The emperor commanded Hilary to return to Gaul. Hilary displayed prompt obedience, but he published in the following year, A.D. 365, an epistle, in which he warned the faithful against Auxentius, against whom he certainly made out a strong case. We do not, after this, hear of any more intercourse between Hilary and the authorities of the State.

But, although the "Athanasius of Gaul" (as M. de Broglie justly calls Hilary) thus came momentarily across the path of a Julian at the commencement of his episcopate, and a Valentinian at its close, the real representative of the State with whom Hilary had dealings was Constantius the Second. The negotia-

F 2

tions between the two lasted for five years (356–361), and were of, a far more elaborately controversial character than Hilary's dealings with Julian or with Valentinian.   Indeed, we have three long letters addressed by Hilary to this sovereign.   This summary of the facts of the case will, it is hoped, be thought to justify the limitation employed in the heading of the present chapter.

Constantius was a man who may fairly claim, perhaps, to be credited with good intentions, but it cannot be said that his ways of carrying them out were either wise or charitable.   He seems to have cherished really strong convictions on behalf of the Christian religion as against heathenism.   But he thought fit to turn against paganism the weapons of persecution which it had employed against the faith of the Cross.   It is true that such force as he did employ was, for the most part, gentle, as compared with the savage deeds of a Nero, a Decius, or a Galerius; nor did the heathens of that age furnish any martyrs for their creed.   Nevertheless, in thus changing the situation, Constantius was robbing the Church of Christ of one of her chief glories.   She could no longer say that violence had again and again been employed against her, but never on her behalf.   Her annalists are almost all agreed in condemning the sort of protection granted by Constantius as both wrong in principle and in every point of view a grave mistake.

The emperor, however, not only believed that severe laws against pagan modes of divination, the overthrow of heathen temples, and excessive im-

munities granted to the clergy, formed a genuine
service to the faith, but he claimed in return the
right of meddling largely with doctrine and with the
controversies then rife concerning it.   For secular
rule he had some real gifts.   Like his father, Constantine, he was skilled in military exercises; like
him he could endure fatigue, was temperate in his
repasts, and of unblemished moral character.   But
he was fussy and self-important; apparently all the
more so, because he was conscious of a want of dignity of presence, being small of stature and slightly
deformed in his legs.   It was observed, that in public
he would refrain from any gesture that might seem to
compromise the stateliness he tried to affect, and
would not so much as cough.   He liked to display
his taste for literature and for theology, and would
indulge his courtiers with long harangues.

As Constantius was only one-and-twenty at the
decease of his father in A.D. 337, some allowance
might well be made for the vanity of one who found
himself at so early an age in a position so exalted.
But the increase of years and of experience did not
in his case bring with it real growth of mind.   No
true largeness of ideas nor firmness of resolution
marked the sway of Constantius.   He did, indeed,
pass by, without retaliation or notice, some very
vehement and insulting addresses to him, more especially those from the pen of Lucifer of Cagliari.   But
he was fond of acting upon secret informations, which
the accused person could not answer; he was too
often the prey of the last courtiers who had access to
his ear.   Among Christians the Arians were eminently

successful in obtaining his favour, and, though that
favour might prove fitful and inconstant, he persecuted at the same time the heathen on one side,
and the defenders of the Catholic faith upon the
other.

Consequently, it is not surprising that neither with
historian, ancient or modern, believing or heathen,
does the memory of Constantius the Second find
grace.   Ammianus and Gibbon are as severe as
Socrates and Döllinger.   Such was the imperial ruler
with whom Hilary was specially confronted.

The three letters to which reference has been made
were respectively addressed by Hilary to Constantius
in the years 355, 360, 361.

The first of the three is a plea for the toleration of
the orthodox against the persecutions being inflicted
upon them by the Arians—persecutions of a character
both coarse and cruel.   It appeared just after the
bishops, led by Hilary, had taken the bold step of
separating themselves from the communion of Valens,
Ursacius, and Saturninus.   A critic of our day, who
is no mean judge of such a matter, calls attention to
the   skill,   the   tact   and   knowledge   of   the   world
displayed   in   the   commencement   of   this   epistle.[1]
Hilary begins by assuring the emperor of the thorough
political submission of the Gauls to his sceptre.

"All is calm," he writes, "amongst us ; no per-
verse or factious proposals are heard ; there is no
suspicion of sedition ; hardly a murmur is audible.
We are living in peace and obedience. . . . . . One

---

[1] The Duc de Broglie.

thing only do we demand of your excellency—it is
that those who have been sent into exile and into the
depths of the deserts, those excellent priests, worthy
of the name which they bear, may be permitted to
return to their homes ; and thus everywhere may
reign liberty and joy."

This language may remind us that Hilary had
begun public life as a magistrate and a statesman.
Even on political grounds, Hilary urges, the emperor
is making a mistake. Among his Catholic subjects
will be found the best defenders of the realm against
internal sedition within, or barbarian invasion from
without. He then proceeds to employ rather the
tone of the philosopher :—

"You toil, O emperor; you govern the state by
wise laws ; you watch day and night, in order that
all under your rule shall enjoy the blessing of liberty.
. . . . God also has brought man to know Him by
His teaching, but has not compelled him to do so by
force. Inspiring respect for His commands through
the admiration of His heavenly marvels, He disdains
the homage of a will that was compelled to confess
Him. If such constraint were employed, even in
support of the true faith, the wisdom of the bishops
would arrest it, and would say : ' *God is Lord of all ;
He has no need of an unwilling allegiance ; He will
have no compulsory confession of faith ; we are not to
deceive, but to serve, Him ; it is for our own sakes,
more than for His, that we are to worship Him.*' I
can only receive him who comes willingly ; I can
only listen to him who prays, and mark with the sign
of the Cross him who believes in it. *We must seek*

after God in simplicity of heart, reverence Him in fear, and worship Him in sincerity of will. Who has ever heard of priests compelled to serve God by chains and punishment ?"

Moderate as this language may seem, it was not such as Constantius was in the habit of hearing. Probably, if he had at the moment been governing Gaul in person, Hilary would at once have been made sensible of the emperor's annoyance ; but Julian, to whose charge the province had been intrusted, was busy in a camp at Vienne on the Rhone. He expected an attack of barbarians, and was wholly engaged in making preparation for the first of those successful campaigns which he subsequently waged against the Alemanni and the Franks. Saturninus of Arles gathered together at Beziers (then known as *Biterra*) a small number of his partisans, and at last, through the intervention of Constantius, obtained from the hands of Julian the formal document which rendered Hilary an exile in Phrygia.

This event, as we have observed, took place at the close of A.D. 356. The second letter of Hilary to Constantius was written fully four years later. It embodies a protest on Hilary's part of innocence of all the charges which, he hears, are brought against him. He is still, he tells Constantius, for all practical purposes a bishop in Gaul, for his clergy listen to his injunctions, and through these he still ministers to his flock. He would gladly meet, in presence of the emperor, the man whom he regards as the real author of his exile, Saturninus, the bishop of Arles, and would like to be allowed to plead for the faith at the council which is about to be summoned (this is the council which ultimately met at Seleucia in A.D. 359). Meanwhile he is deeply conscious of the injury wrought to Christianity by the clashing of rival councils and varying professions of faith.

The emperor appears to have been anxious to see a creed drawn up which should not contain any phrase which was not to be found in Holy Scripture. This was a marked feature of the Semi-Arian case, and it must be owned that it is at first sight a highly plausible one; but it will not bear examination, for the very point at issue was what meaning was to be attached to this or that expression of Scripture. No commentator would be willing to be limited to the precise phraseology of the author whose writings he is trying to explain. As a plain matter of fact, at the present time it would be impossible to name any Christian community which has found itself able to act upon this theory. To carry it out in its integrity would almost require the employment of the original languages in which the Scriptures were written; for a translation, as even a beginner in scholarship must be aware, very often almost of necessity partakes of the nature of a commentary.

The Arians themselves do not seem to have urged this plea. Indeed, on their part it would have been transparently absurd, for they had a whole class of watchwords, of which not one was to be found in Scripture—as, for instance, the phrases specially condemned in the earliest edition of the Nicene Creed. Even on the part of the Semi-Arians it was inconsistent, for they, too, clung to the non-Scriptural term, *homöousion*, quite as persistently as their opponents did to their watchword.

Such is substantially the comment of Hilary upon the emperor's demand. He praises Constantius for his anxiety that his faith should be Scriptural, but he maintains that this is precisely what he and his friends are trying to teach. Only Constantius ought to remember, that all those whom even he would denounce as heretics make precisely the same claim. The emperor's allies had denounced, for example, Photinus and Sabellius; but Photinus and Sabellius both averred that their tenets were Scriptural. Montanus, who had employed the ministry of women who were apparently mad, had made the same claim. "They all talk Scripture without the sense of Scripture, and without true faith set forth a faith."

Thus far the addresses of Hilary to Constantius had been, it is admitted on all sides, loyal, respectful, and thoroughly Christian in tone. " It would be unjust," says a writer, who is by no means unduly favourable to champions of orthodoxy, "not to acknowledge the beautiful and Christian sentiments scattered throughout his two former addresses to Constantius, which are firm but respectful ; and, if rigidly, yet sincerely dogmatic. His plea for toleration, if not consistently maintained, is expressed with great force and simplicity."[1]

The words just cited, of course, imply a reference to the third letter. It must have been written a year

---

[1] Milman, "History of Christianity," book iii., chap. v.

after the date (A.D. 360) in which the second was presented to the emperor.

During this time Constantius appears to have changed his plans. Hitherto, though not inflicting death upon any of the orthodox, he had employed the punishment of exile with great recklessness. Bishops in all directions had been dismissed, as has been observed, from their sees—we have abundant evidence besides Hilary's on this point — without much care as to the district named. Thus Paulinus, bishop of Trèves, a man of high and holy character, having been banished into an heretical district, had been driven to beg for bread. Moreover, some of their faithful presbyters had been compelled to work in the mines.

Nevertheless, it seems probable that, if Constantius had continued to pursue this policy, Hilary, though he issued protests and petitions (far more for others than for himself), might have continued to address Constantius in comparatively moderate language. He had apparently a strong conviction that such punishments wrought their own cure, were often over-ruled to good, and ultimately did injury to the cause of those Arians who sympathised with the emperor in his action and had in some cases (as in Hilary's own) apparently suggested the victims.

But the emperor in the last years of his life—he died in A.D. 361—adopted a much more conciliatory policy. It was an illustration, to some extent, of the fable about the wind and the sun contending for the traveller's cloak. Invitations to the palace, bribes, good dinners, imperial flatteries were freely lavished; and it seems to have been found that many who would have been proof against harsh measures were really influenced by these allurements.

On almost the only occasion in his life of which we have any evidence, Hilary now thoroughly abandoned the tone of moderation which he generally employed. Constantius, by this change of policy, became in his eyes the worst of enemies to the truth; a very Antichrist, who would fain make the world a present to Satan. He appeals to the evidences of his own former moderation; but the time for gentleness has gone by. For his part he would thankfully see back again the time when the little-horse and the stocks, the fire and the axe, were plied against the faith of the Cross.

" But now we are contending against a deceitful persecutor, against a flattering enemy, against an Antichrist Constantius, who does not scourge the back, but pampers the appetite; who does not issue proscriptions that lead us to immortal life, but rich gifts that betray to endless death; does not send us from prison to liberty, but loads us inside the palace with honours that bribe to slavery; does not torture the body, but makes himself master of the heart; does not strike off heads with the sword, but slays the soul with gold; does not in public threaten with fire, but in secret is kindling for us a hell; does not aim at true self-conquest, but flatters that he may lord it over us; confesses Christ for the purpose of denying Him; aims at unity for the destruction of true peace; represses heresies, but in such wise as

would leave no Christians ; honours priests, that he
may do away with bishops ; and builds the Church's
walls, that he may destroy her faith."

Then presently, with fresh vehemence, but with
perhaps some measure of inconsistency, Hilary proceeds to accuse Constantius of, at least, some partial
and local persecution of a more direct character :—

" To thee, O Constantius, do I proclaim what I
would have uttered before Nero, what Decius and
Maximin would have heard from me.   Thou art
warring against God, raging against the Church, per-
secuting the Saints.   Thou hatest those that preach
Christ, thou art overthrowing religion, tyrant as thou
art, no longer merely in things human, but in things
divine. . . . A doctor art thou of lore profane, and,
untaught in real piety, thou art giving bishoprics to
thine allies, and changing good ones for bad ; thou
art committing priests to prison, thou arrayest thine
armies to strike terror into the Church ; thou closest
synods and compellest the faith of the Orientals to
become impiety.   Those who are shut up in one city
thou dost frighten with threats, weaken by famine,
kill with cold, mislead by dissimulation.   So, most
wicked of mortal men, dost thou manipulate all the
ills of persecution, as to shut out the chance of
pardon in the event of sin, and of martyrdom where
there is confessorship.   This hath that father of thine,
that murderer from the beginning, taught thee—how
to prevail without insult, to stab without the sword,
to persecute without infamy, to indulge hatred without being suspected, to lie without being discovered,
to make professions of faith while in unbelief, to

flatter without kindliness, to act, carry out your own will, while yet concealing that will."

This letter has not unnaturally been the one special object of attack with those who are inclined to lower Hilary. Men, who have no strong convictions of their own, imply that *they* would have always kept their temper under similar circumstances. But it is far less easy to judge such cases fairly than might at first sight be supposed. Sarcasm and invective almost always seem lawful weapons when employed on our own side; then they are just reproof and holy indignation. But turned against us they look like irreverence, and seem to carry with them their own condemnation. "If," as Möhler remarks, concerning the case before us,—"if we drive men to despair, we ought to be prepared to hear them speak the language of despair."

Even those who, while sympathising in the main with Hilary, may think his language excessive, and that he would have been wiser to preserve his more usual tone, must allow that his excess was not on that side to which men are generally most tempted. From the pagan orators of the day Constantius heard nothing but the language of flattery—flattery which on their part could not possibly have been sincere. And when we remember to how many teachers of religion undue subservience to the great has at some time of their life proved a snare—a list including men so different as Martin Luther, Laud, Bourdaloue—when we think of the special temptations of our own Church and age, we ought to make some allowance even for the excesses of those who have, at least, been preserved from what Bishop Andrewes teaches us to pray, " from making gods of kings."

We have given the very fiercest passages of this celebrated epistle, because neither on this nor on any other topic in Hilary's career do we wish to conceal anything. How far it is censurable in point of temper and of wisdom will always probably remain a point on which men must be content to differ. But two or three features of the case to which we have already made partial reference deserve some further consideration before we pass a judgment on it.

In the first place, Hilary, as a student of classic literature, was probably (though Quintilian was his favourite author) more or less familiar with the speeches of the greatest of Roman orators. Now, the eloquence of Cicero is certainly not always free from gross personalities ; he can be, says one of his latest editors—Mr. Long—" most foul-mouthed." There are passages in the oration which Juvenal selects as Cicero's grandest effort, the second Philippic against Mark Antony, which are far more insulting than any sentences of Hilary ; and it would be easy to multiply examples of this fault. Many of the readers of the epistle to Constantius would, more or less consciously, judge the document as a piece of Roman literature, and from such a point of view it would not greatly startle or astonish them.

But this, it will be said, is to put out of sight that Hilary was not a Roman consul, but a Christian bishop. The answer to such a charge shall be stated in the language of a living English judge : " It must also be borne in mind that, though Christianity ex-

presses the tender and charitable sentiments with
such passionate ardour, it has also a terrible side."[1]
Gentleness is not its only characteristic. There are
times when not only the seers of old, but the Prophet
of prophets, found stern objurgation a necessity.
Remove all such elements from the Gospel records,
and they become at once a different book. If, then,
the possibility of need for such reproof is proved by
the highest and holiest of all examples, we may
indeed question the manner or the degree in which it
has been followed by Christ's servants, but we must not
say that it is in itself necessarily wrong or unneeded.

There is one more consideration which specially
applies to English Churchmen. All systems and
communions, even those of divine origin, being human
in their working, must needs possess their weak sides.
Now, it is to be feared that the accusation made
against the Anglican communion of an undue leaning
towards the side of temporal authority is not without
some real foundation. The charge, though since reite-
rated by foes, has been made by more than one of her
own sons. Careful study of our own faults, and
earnest desire to amend them, are amongst the best
pledges, under divine favour, for amendment alike in
individuals and in societies. We may not have anything to show in this direction so deplorable as the
flattery of Louis XIV. by the great French preachers
of his age ; but in this matter Anglicanism is not
blameless. Let us, then, bethink ourselves whether,
since the present so deeply influences our judgments

[1] "Liberty, Equality, Fraternity," by the Hon. Mr. Justice
Stephen.

on the past, we may not unconsciously be inclined to judge with injustice those who have found themselves in a position of resistance to constituted authority in the State.

What, in effect, would have been produced upon the mind of Constantius by the letter of Hilary, we cannot tell. Gibbon describes the character of the emperor as a compound " of pride and weakness, of superstition and cruelty." But Constantius had, nevertheless, shown considerable indifference to written attacks, and might possibly have judged silence to be in this case also the wisest course. At the moment, however, when the letter was published, Constantius was dying, perhaps actually dead. He expired, after a short illness, on the 3rd of November, A.D. 361, in Asia Minor, not many miles from Tarsus, and was succeeded by his nephew, the gifted and too celebrated Julian.

CHAPTER X.

MISTAKES OF HILARY.

THOSE who are at all familiar, even as bystanders, with the practice of law-courts, may frequently have observed the presence of the following well-known element of discussion. Counsel on one side refer to some *dictum* of a distinguished judge, such as a Lord Hardwick or Lord Stowell, as involving a clear anticipation of the cause now being debated, and as virtually guiding the court in the direction of a particular decision. It is replied on the other side that no one questions the great weight which is given to the rulings of the high authority just cited, nor its application to the point which is now mooted. But, it is added, the sentence does not occur in the actual decision of a matter duly argued before the judge and pronounced upon accordingly. It only comes in incidentally, perhaps, by way of illustration; and it is obvious that the judge had never brought all the powers of his mind to bear upon the subject. It is merely a saying by the way, or, in the Latin phraseology which is commonly applied to it, an *obiter dictum*. Under such circumstances it is justly felt that the weight of the pronouncement is greatly lessened.

Now this principle is one of wide extent. It is applicable to inquiries into the rulings of scientific

authorities and to general literature. To few departments of study is it more applicable than to the field
of patristic literature; and Hilary of Poitiers is certainly one of those thinkers whose writings call for
an equitable and charitable consideration from this
especial point of view.

On four main themes Hilary must be pronounced
to have been eminently successful. They are as follows :—First comes his natural and suggestive style
of commentary on Holy Scripture, more particularly
on the Book of Psalms and the Gospel according to St.
Matthew. In the second place, he deserves a place
among those who have given us highly interesting and
valuable information concerning the mental process
whereby they were led from the errors of paganism
into the acceptance of the Christian faith,—a place
less exalted perhaps than that of some other Fathers
(as, for example, St. Justin Martyr and St. Augustine),
but, nevertheless, a very high one. Thirdly, he is
great in delineation of the spiritual nature of the
Godhead as opposed to the dark and often degrading
perversions into which the heathen nations had fallen.
And, lastly, as has already been implied, he is a
champion (we may say in the west, *the* champion) for
the great dogmas of the full and perfect Divinity of
our Lord and Saviour and the Holy Trinity in Unity.
Some faint idea of his work in these four departments
we trust to be able to give, through extracts, in a
succeeding chapter.

But there were some other very important ques
tions concerning the union of two natures in the One
Person of the adorable Lord, of the completeness of

His manhood, and of the way in which He redeemed
us, which had not, in the age of Hilary, received the
amount of attention which their interest and importance would seem to invite.   It is important to bear
this in mind, if we would judge any of the early Fathers
with fairness.   Our own creed on these points is made
up of a number of elements welded together.   It is
not easy to name anywhere a more masterly statement
concerning the Incarnate Lord than the one given in
the second of the Thirty-nine Articles.   But those
brief and balanced sentences are the outcome of many
struggles.   Not only Arius, but also Nestorius and
Eutyches, have contributed towards them, in that by
their respective heresies they necessitated this formu-
lation of the true doctrine with the aid of Athanasius
and Hilary, of Cyril and of Leo.   Nor is this all.   It
is hardly too much to say that the view of the Atone-
ment most ordinarily taught amongst us is, *in its
form*, a mediæval doctrine.   It is, in the main, as
Archbishop Thomson has pointed out, the theory of
Anselm, elaborated and improved by Aquinas.[1]   Now,
Anselm was archbishop of Canterbury in the reign of
William Rufus, at the close of the eleventh century
(A.D. 1097), and Aquinas wrote in the middle of the
thirteenth century, at least 150 years later.

Besides a few incidental mistakes (such as the
supposition that Moses, like Elias, was still alive),
Hilary seems at times to fail in grasping the doctrine
that our Lord took His human nature from the Virgin
Mother, of her substance, and to miss the distinction

---

[1] "Bampton Lectures" for 1853, p. 166.

implied in the words, that, although He who is God
the Son suffered, yet the Godhead did not suffer. In
his anxiety to refute the Arians, he appears, at least in
one passage of his treatise, "De Trinitate" (lib. x.),
not merely to represent the Deity as impassible, but
to deny the reality of our Lord's sufferings. It is possible that he did not really mean this, and certainly
other parts of his writings look the other way.
Nevertheless, the language of the "De Trinitate"
must be regarded as incautious, and as demanding
considerable charity of interpretation.

Such mistakes must needs appear to us all the
more strange, because the doctrines, to which reference has just been made, not only come before us
as a part of the heritage of the Church universal,
but also find expression of a clear and emphatic kind
in Holy Scripture. Thus, to take but one passage
out of many, the language of St. Paul, "God sent
forth His Son, made of a woman,"[1] is decisive on one
point; and the texts in the writings of the prophets,
in the Gospels and in the Epistles, which dwell upon
the importance of the sufferings of Christ as an
essential part of His atoning work, are as abundant
as they are pathetic and wonderful. But it must
be borne in mind, that in the age of Hilary the
canon of the New Testament was barely settled.
Indeed, Hilary's great compeer and fellow-champion,
Athanasius, was the first bishop who is known to have
issued to his diocese a list of the books recognised
and read in Church canonical scriptures. Hilary

---

[1] Galatians iv. 4. On the second point it may be enough to
refer to Psalm xxii. and Isaiah liii. as specially emphatic.

was living in a somewhat out-of-the-way part of Christendom. Up to the eve of his banishment he had never heard the Nicene Creed, though he had taught its doctrines,[1] and it may well have happened that some portions of the New Testament were less well known to him than others. But, even if this were not the case, it must probably be admitted that sympathetic appreciation of our Lord's sufferings was brought out more strongly in the mediæval than in the patristic ages. This would only be one illustration out of many of the correctness of the language of the historian, Evagrius, and of St. Augustine, as also of a well-known passage in Bishop Butler's "Analogy,"[2] to the effect that knowledge in things divine has been attained in the past, and will be attained in the future "in the same way as natural knowledge is come at, by the continuance and progress of learning and liberty, and by particular persons attending to, comparing, and pursuing intimations scattered up and down the Scripture, which are overlooked and disregarded by the generality of the world." For the same reason, namely, that it had not yet been debated, the language of Hilary concerning the Holy Spirit seems less clear and emphatic than is desirable.

On the whole, it seems reasonable to consider that

---

[1] "After my baptism, and indeed after I had dwelt as bishop some time in my diocese, I had never heard the Nicene Creed." —Hilary, "On Synods," cap. xci. He had heard it just as he was going into exile; but he had steadily taught the doctrine set forth in it.

[2] "Analogy of Religion," part ii., chap. iii.

the two principal mistakes of Hilary were of such
a nature that they would have become very grave
and serious, and have imperilled the purity of the
faith, if they had been clearly reasoned out and
insisted upon by him. But this never came to pass :
they were not, at the moment when he wrote, *the*
questions at issue. Moreover, it is highly probable
that in a later generation, when the errors of Nestorius became manifest, Hilary would have perceived
his mistakes, and have proved willing to explain and
to retract. As against the deadly heresies of his
own day, he must ever be acknowledged as a confessor ; as a great, and, under God's good providence,
a highly successful champion.

CHAPTER XI.

THE CRITICS OF HILARY.

IF the career of a man, who has been eminent in the world of thought and of action, has confessedly been marked by some outbursts of vehemence and some errors of judgment, we must expect to find at least two lines of criticism adopted concerning him. There will be those who, having only a half liking, or possibly even an antipathy, to the cause represented by him, will dwell most upon the defects; there will be others who, without positively denying the failings or mistakes, will regard them as the proverbial spots upon the sun, the incidents of human frailty which may virtually be ignored, in consideration of the trials which he underwent and the noble service which he rendered.

Hilary of Poitiers so lived and so wrote that we might expect beforehand to meet with such a variety of opinion as that above indicated. In his case, the decision depends more, perhaps, upon temperament than upon the ecclesiastical position of the critics. The Protestant Daillé is among those who judge Hilary with severity; the Protestant Dorner is enthusiastic in his admiration. Erasmus, who, despite all that he effected on behalf of the Reformation, ultimately remained Roman Catholic, certainly gives full weight, to say the least, to what may be regarded as the blemishes of Hilary's writings ; other Roman Catholics, as the Benedictine editor and the charitable Möhler, see the bright side only, and ignore or excuse whatever has been urged by the assailants.

Gibbon declares, that "Erasmus, with admirable sense and freedom, has delineated the just character of Hilary."[1] This is, in our estimation, a rather excessive eulogy. However, the opinions of such a man as Erasmus must always deserve consideration ; and we propose, as fairly as we can, to give a brief account of his essay on Hilary, and to attempt to rate it at its true value. Possibly, even Erasmus himself, if he had known Gibbon, might have considered praise from such a quarter a slightly questionable gift.

Erasmus declares that editors had in many places modified the language of Hilary in order to make it seem more orthodox. In some cases of this kind noted by Erasmus, the language of Hilary is quite defensible ; and it does seem that Hilary himself would have been the last person to claim infallibility for his writings. " Such felicity," writes Erasmus, " God willed to be peculiar to the sacred Scriptures only. Outside these, no man, however learned and keen-sighted, is free from occasional lapses and blindness ; to the end that all might remember that they are but men, and should be read by us as men with discrimination, with judgment, and, at the same time,

---

[1] "Decline and Fall," chap. xxi., note 64.

with charity." Hilary, in the opinion of Erasmus, hesitated for some time before throwing in his lot with the cause of the Athanasian and the Nicene Creeds. Possibly, says the critic, he thought it a good cause, but hopeless ; possibly he had not fully made up his own mind. To us the latter of these theories seems not only the more charitable, but infinitely the more probable of the two.

The " De Trinitate" is the book, says Erasmus, on which Hilary lavished all his strength. It stands to his mind in the same relation in which the Georgics do to that of Virgil, the story of Medea to that of Ovid, the " De Oratore" to that of Cicero, and the " De Civitate Dei" to that of St. Augustine. In the judgment of Erasmus, there are parts of this work which approach the borders of a dangerous curiosity. Now this must always be a profoundly difficult problem. Who is to draw the line between what is, and what is not, lawful speculation in things divine ? The stricture of Erasmus is a far-reaching one, and it may be reasonably doubted whether he was quite the man to make it. How greatly the judgments of good and wise men may differ in such matters may be illustrated by a single instance. We are accustomed in England to hear a famous divine of the Elizabethan age spoken of as " the judicious Hooker." Yet, not only has the correctness of the title been questioned by Coleridge, but a more trustworthy critic, an eminent English bishop of our time, has expressed the opinion, that parts of Hooker's fifth book may possibly be thought to go beyond the bounds of safe speculation.

Erasmus, while wishing that theological learning would restrain its definitions within the bounds of Scripture (a somewhat ambiguous expression),[1] yet admits that even in apostolic times it was heresy that led to fresh expressions of truth (the Cerinthians and Ebionites having necessitated the composition of the Gospel of St. John), and, ultimately, to the formation of creeds. In the case of controversy, says Erasmus, we must make allowance for men being carried away. Thus Tertullian, waxing fierce against some divines of his day who were paying too much honour to matrimony, rushed into the opposite extreme. The language of St. Jerome on the same subject is indefensible, if it be judged with strictness. St. Augustine, warring with all his energies against Pelagius, assigned considerably less to our free will[2] than do the reigning theologians of our day, that is to say, the fifteenth century.

These remarks of Erasmus appear to be just and fair. In relation to Tertullian and Jerome, it may be alleged (as a gifted and eloquent lecturer of our time has said) that in certain ages there was a fanaticism of the ascetic principle, in another age a fanaticism of scholarship, while in our own day there appears to

[1] It is ambiguous for this reason, that the question so often turns on the precise meaning of the terms of Scripture. Certainly no sectaries ever had a fuller repertory of non-Scriptural watchwords than the Arians, Semi-Arians, and Anomœans.

[2] I render *liberum arbitrium* by the words free will, not as forgetting the objections of Locke to the phrase, but because it seems, in popular estimation, to survive and practically triumph over those objections.

be in some quarters danger of a fanaticism of physical science. The remark of Erasmus in reference to St. Augustine would certainly meet with large acceptance, alike in the nineteenth as in the fifteenth century.

But Erasmus passes on to the application of these remarks to Hilary. In the first place he censures the vehemence of his language against the Arians. We are not inclined to defend it ; but it must be observed that Hilary had to deal with a peculiarly treacherous and aggravating specimen of Arians in the case of Auxentius of Milan, and still more so in that of Saturninus of Arles. If all wielders of such weapons—and, after all, they are but occasional with Hilary—are to be struck out of the list of those who have rendered signal benefit to the Church, that list must be considerably reduced. That it was the men themselves, and the whole tone and spirit of their warfare, that provoked Hilary is clear from the great difference of his attitude towards the Semi-Arians. If it be urged that such palliation is only a result of the theological hatred (*odium theologicum*) of all time, it must be replied that the Arians fare but little better in this respect in the pages of writers by no means conspicuous for love of orthodoxy. It is sufficient to refer the student who questions this assertion to the works of Dean Milman, and even of Gibbon.

But a further objection on the part of Erasmus affects the fame, not of Hilary merely, but of the Church at large. The struggle, says Erasmus, concerned matters far removed from the grasp of human intellect. To this it must be replied that, as there may be a false charity, and a false justice, so, too, there may be such a thing as a false ignorance. Christians believe that God has given them a revelation, and that in essential points the meaning of that revelation can be proved. The great fact remains, that while the endlessly shifting creeds of the Arians and their allies have perished, the Nicene Creed, for which Athanasius and Hilary contended, is still an honoured and valued portion of the heritage of Christendom, still holds its place as a part of the highest act of Christian worship.

If I, says Erasmus, had lived in the time of Hilary, I would have uttered warnings and teachings against the Arians, but I would not have called them Satans or Antichrists.

We are all, more or less, creatures of our age. Most assuredly, in few instances, is this more manifest than in the life and character of Erasmus. He was a product of two great movements, the *Renaissance* and the *Reformation*. From the former he derived the keen and polished style of his admirable Latinity; from the latter his spirit of assault upon the corruptions of the Roman Catholic system. An Erasmus of the fourth century can hardly be imagined. Thus much, however, we may safely concede to him. If he could have been a contemporary of Hilary, Erasmus would not have written with vehemence against the Arians, it was not in his nature to do so; but we should have had from his pen keen, incisive satires on their writings, their proceedings, their relations with the Court, the fluctuations and inconsistencies of their multitudinous creeds. On some minds the weapons thus wielded would have produced more effect than any amount of hard names and vehement protestations. To others they would have seemed far more exasperating. But, just as Principal Robertson has remarked, that of the abuses thundered against by Luther, there was hardly one that had not been previously satirised by Erasmus, so, probably, it would have been in the fourth century. An Erasmus of that date, if such a personage could have existed, would have left denunciation to Hilary of Poitiers, to Lucifer of Cagliari, and a few more ; but his own share in the contest, however prominent, would have taken another turn, and have been of a different kind.

But, continues Erasmus, if, in the writings of Hilary himself, some want of grasp on the Person of the Holy Spirit, on the derivation of our Lord's human nature from the Virgin Mother, and on other points of importance seem to require a charitable interpreter, what right had such an author to speak so vehemently of the errors of others?

There is certainly force in this consideration. More light, more knowledge of weak points in his own theology, might have induced Hilary, and many more before and since, to be more guarded in their language towards opponents. Still, it must be granted, that on few points are we all more likely to be prejudiced than in the matter of satire and of invective. When used upon our own side they seem most lawful weapons, justified by the attitude of an Elijah towards the priests of Baal, by St. Paul towards the Corinthians, by a higher and holier example in the censure of the Scribes and Pharisees. But when we find them turned against our friends, or against the supporters of a cause we cherish, they then become mere headlong temper or irreverence. Assuredly, to refer to a single illustration, the wit of the " Provincial Letters " of Blaise Pascal appeared to his Jansenist allies the most legitimate of instruments ; but against his Jesuit opponents he had to defend the style which he adopted. In like manner the language on opposite sides of a Calvin and a Maldonatus, of a Wicliff and his adversaries, will be viewed differently by members of reformed and unreformed communions.

Erasmus says that there may have been good and pious Arians, sincerely convinced that they were right. Hilary might at least reply, that he *had* met such men among the Semi-Arians, and had treated them with the respect and courtesy which they deserved, but that his personal experience of Arian opponents had been the very reserve of the imaginary portraiture made by his critic.

Erasmus considers that, in his commentary upon St. Matthew, Hilary has too freely adopted the allegorical mode of interpretation pursued by that great genius Origen, from whom he borrowed largely. This is very possible ; but to draw the exact line of demarcation between lawful and unlawful use of allegory is a task of much depth and difficulty, on which we cannot here pretend to enter further than protest against any such employment of it as would explain away the historic truth of the great events of our Lord's human career, His birth, His crucifixion, His resurrection, and His ascension.

Of the judgment of Erasmus on another point of less importance, namely, the question of style, we have already spoken. The fastidious taste of Erasmus —unquestionably a master of elegant expression—is slightly dissatisfied with Hilary. He thinks that Hilary is wanting in severe simplicity ; that in translating from Greek authors he infused a grandiloquence to which Gallic authors of that day were somewhat prone. However, Erasmus admits that Hilary's style has marked individuality. Moreover, as regards want of simplicity, he errs in good company, for his critic considers that scarcely any provincial writers of Latin, save a few who had lived at Rome from boyhood, can be acquitted of faultiness in this respect.

Curiously enough, Erasmus does not find any fault with the vehement letter against Constantius, but is inclined to think the previous epistles to the emperor to be slightly reticent and over-courtly.

He has pointed out the faults of Hilary, he declares, not in order to dim the glory and insult the reputation of a most holy and learned man, but for a warning to the bishops and theologians of his own day. Some defenders of the Papacy in his time are quite outrageous, and call a man a schismatic if he detract anything from the authority of the Bishop of Rome. We could ill spare the works of Origen and Tertullian, Chrysostom and Jerome, Augustine and Hilary, nor are even Aquinas and Scotus, says Erasmus, wholly out of date. The authority of Hilary is evidently ranked by Jerome even above that of Ambrose and

Augustine. At any rate (says our censor in conclusion), he was a great man, and his chief work displays genius, eloquence, and great knowledge of Holy Scripture.

It may seem, perhaps, as if this chapter ought to have been headed " A Critic of Hilary " ; and it is true that it has been almost exclusively devoted to the opinions of Erasmus. No other writer, save the Benedictine editor, has gone so fully into detail. But we turn from the strictures of one who, with all his merits, is inclined to be rather carping and fastidious, and proceed to set down the more generous if less critical testimonies of some primitive and modern authorities.

Here, for example, is the judgment of St. Augustine, written about A.D. 400, concerning Hilary :— " An illustrious doctor of the Churches. A man of no light authority in explanation of the Scriptures and assertion of the faith. A keen defender of the Catholic Church against heretics."

St. Augustine's learned and gifted contemporary, St. Jerome, is even more emphatic in his eulogies. Alluding to the former eminence of some divines in secular station, Jerome asks : " Do not that holy and most eloquent man, the martyr Cyprian, and Hilary, a confessor of our own age, look like men who were once like lofty trees in this world's garden, but who afterwards built up the Church of God ? " Elsewhere Jerome speaks of Hilary as "the Rhone of eloquence . . . one in whose writings the piety of the faith never wavers. . . . A man whose writings I have traversed, and found no stumbling-blocks for my feet."

H

If the consent of those who in many respects are at variance adds weight to testimony, the evidence of an antagonist of Jerome, Rufinus, becomes important. Now Rufinus calls Hilary "a confessor of the Catholic faith," and adds, that "his book against Auxentius is one of most ample information."

Some fifty years later (i.e. about A.D. 450) we find the ecclesiastical historian, Socrates, describing the efforts made by ·Eusebius, bishop of Vercelli, in company with Hilary, to oppose the progress of Arianism in North Italy. "These two," writes Socrates, "strove nobly side by side for the faith. Moreover, Hilary, who was an eloquent man, set forth in his books in the Latin language, the dogmas of *The One Substance*, and powerfully confuted the Arian dogmas." The learned Benedictine, Dom Ceillier, is also entirely on the favourable side.

In the Middle Ages the best construction was placed upon any doubtful expressions of Hilary by the first occupant of the see of Canterbury after the Norman Conquest, the illustrious Lanfranc; by the author of the famous "Four Books of Sentences," Peter Lombard, bishop of Paris; and by the greatest of the schoolmen, St. Thomas Aquinas. This statement implies, what is no doubt the case, that some critics had been less favourable. But with the exception of an early one, Claudianus Mamertus, they were not men of mark.

Since the Reformation the Gallican historian, M. Noel Alexandre (better known by his Latinised appellation of Natalis Alexander) may be named among the apologists for Hilary; and a still more energetic

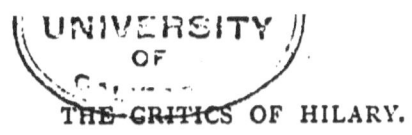

defender, the Benedictine editor of his works, Dom Coutant. The Anglican, Cave, is also favourable.

Coming down to our own century, we find among the severe critics of Hilary the rationalistic Baur of Tubingen. But in the opposite camp stand devout and careful thinkers, both among ourselves, as Canons Bright and Robertson, and also among Roman Catholics and Protestants on the Continent. The Duc de Broglie in his "Church and Empire in the Fourth Century," justly entitles Hilary "the Athanasius of Gaul," and, as we have seen, calls attention to his tact and knowledge of the world as well as to his loftier qualities. Another Roman Catholic, the learned and charitable Möhler, had previously, in his "Athanasius the Great," given a brief comment on the aid afforded to the famous Bishop of Alexandria by his brother-bishop of Poitiers. "Thus," writes Möhler, "did St. Hilary develope with ability and depth his ideas on the essence of the faith and its relations with science; on the Catholic Church and its relations with heretics in general, and his own age in particular."

Pope Pius IX., towards the close of his long pontificate, declared Hilary to be a doctor of the universal Church. Our Roman Catholic fellow-Christians do not seem agreed among themselves how much is meant by this title; but it must of course be intended to imply a general recognition of orthodoxy. No one, however, among modern theologians seems to have devoted so much time and attention to the writings of Hilary as the Lutheran Dorner in his deep, original, and learned volumes on "The Doctrine of the Person of Christ." Dorner is enthusiastic in his admiration, possibly too determined to ignore even the slightest blemish in this Father of the fourth century. But his defence deserves deep consideration, because he has studied the writings of Hilary, and especially the " De Trinitate," with such zealous care and sympathy. Anticipating the judgment of Pius IX. by a whole generation, Dorner sums up his analysis of him in the following words, with which we may well conclude the present chapter :—

" Our attention is, above all, attracted to Hilarius of Pictavium. We feel the more drawn to him, because he does not appear hitherto to have met with the consideration he deserves. Hilarius is one of the most difficult Church teachers to understand, but also one of the most original and profound. His view of Christology is one of the most interesting in the whole of Christian antiquity. . . . Hilarius evinced himself to be, in the true sense, a teacher of the Church."

CHAPTER XII.

HILARY AS TEACHER AND AS COMMENTATOR.

IT is high time to let Hilary speak for himself on some of the subjects which he treated. We commence with a few extracts from the first book of his treatise, " De Trinitate," relating to the grounds of his conversion to Christianity, of which we attempted to give a general idea in the first chapter of this volume.

Hilary first lays down and comments on the propo- sition that the happiness which is based on mere ease and abundance cannot be reckoned as much superior to that enjoyed by a considerable portion of the brute creation. Most men of worth have, at any rate, got beyond this point, and have seen both the need of cultivating certain virtues, inasmuch as a good life evidently required good actions and sound under- standing. They have also felt within themselves that it was improbable that a Being Who had bestowed upon us such gifts should have intended that our existence should be bounded by this earthly life. So far—and here Hilary has with him certain earlier con- verts, as, for instance, St. Justin Martyr—he went with the heathen philosophers. Hilary then proceeds as follows :—

" Now, although I did not consider their sentiments

on these points either foolish or useless, when they taught us to keep our consciences free from all fault, and in respect of the troubles of human life to meet them by foresight, avoid them by judgment, or bear them with patience, nevertheless, these men did not seem to me thoroughly competent guides towards the attainment of a good and happy life. The precepts they laid down were obvious ones, and in accordance with good sense. Not to admit them were but brutish, while to grant them and yet not to act upon them would seem like madness, surpassing the senselessness of brutes. But my soul felt a strong impulse not merely to do those things which to leave undone would be alike criminal and a source of woes, but to gain the knowledge of that God Who is the author of all our gifts, to Whom our being owed itself, in the service of Whom it would feel itself ennobled, to Whom it must refer every conception of hope, in Whose goodness it could rest amidst the great troubles of our present condition as if in a safe and most friendly harbour. To understand or to grasp a knowledge of Him my soul was enkindled with a desire that burned within me."

After speaking of the unworthy opinions of the ancients, whether atheistic (denying God), or polytheistic (as of gods many and lords many, degraded by human passions) ; or of a god—and this seemed the most general opinion—who existed, indeed, but was utterly indifferent about the affairs of earth ; of gods in the likeness of cattle or confined within stocks and stones, Hilary proceeds as follows :—

" But my soul, rendered anxious amid such

thoughts, struggled to find a road useful and needful for the attainment of the knowledge of its Lord. It did not recognise as worthy of God a carelessness about things which He had Himself created ; it perceived that sexes in the Godhead, and successions of parents and children, were incompatible with a powerful and imperishable nature; yea, further, it held for certain that what was Divine and Eternal must needs be One and indivisible. For, being the author of its own existence, it must of necessity leave nothing outside it more excellent than itself. Thus, then, almightiness and eternity could be properties of One alone. For in almightiness there could not properly be any ' stronger' or ' weaker'; nor in eternity any 'latter' or 'former,' since in God was nothing to be adored save that which was power and eternity."

In the next section he tells us what he learnt from the Scriptures :—

" While thinking over these and many kindred subjects, I lighted on the books which the religion of the Hebrews has handed down to us as written by Moses and the prophets. In these were contained the following words, whereby the God the Creator testifies concerning Himself: 'I am that I am,' and again : ' Thus shalt Thou say unto the children of Israel, I AM hath sent me unto you.' Much did I marvel at an utterance concerning God which was so complete, which described in language so suitable for the human understanding the incomprehensible knowledge of the divine nature. For of God we perceive that no property can be more specially His than to be ; since the very fact of His existence is the mark

of One Who is never-ending and had no beginning.
That which is everlasting, with the power of blessed-
ness unalloyed, never has been, or will be, able to be
non-existent, since all that is divine is liable neither
to destruction nor to commencement. And, since the
eternity of God never lacketh anything that is needful,
worthily doth He set forth the fact of His being as an
evidence of His own imperishable eternity."

Hilary proceeds to comment upon other passages
of Holy Scripture connected with this theme which
had specially arrested his attention, such as, for example, Isaiah lxvi. 1, 2 ; Psalm cxxxix. To these he
devotes some pages, and shows how, in combination
with a passage from the Book of Wisdom, xiii. 5, they
led him onward to further comprehension of the infinite and omnipresent nature of the Creator and of
the beauty of the Divine Being, as evidenced in the
order and beauty of creation. These thoughts confirmed in his mind that conviction of immortality
which even natural reason had suggested. But the
teachings of the Old Testament were wonderfully
deepened and invigorated by one of the books of the
New Dispensation—the Gospel of St. John. He cites
the well-known verses from the first chapter (the precise passage selected for the Gospel on Christmas
Day), and then makes the following remarks on the
results of studying them :—

" The mind has its intelligence carried beyond the
powers of the natural senses, and learns more than it
heretofore conceived concerning God. It learns that
its Creator is God of God ; it hears that the Word is
God, and was with God in the beginning."

After briefly paraphrasing the remainder of the passage, Hilary proceeds with a fresh section, of which the heading runs thus :—
"The Son of God is God. To become sons of God is a power vouchsafed to us, but not a necessity. The Son of God was made man, that man might be made the son of God. Christ is very God, and very man."

The section proceeds :—
"Here the alarmed and anxious mind finds more hope than it looked for. In the first place, it is tinged with the knowledge of God as a Father; and the conception it formerly entertained through natural reason concerning the eternity, infinity, and beauty of its Maker, it now understands to be the property also of the only-begotten God.[1] It does not relax its faith so as to believe in more gods than one, because it hears of 'God of God.' It does not have recourse to the notion of a diversity of nature between God and God, because it learns that 'God from God' is full of grace and truth ; nor does it imagine any precedence, or the reverse, in point of time, because it finds that God was in the beginning with God."

A little later on he adds :—
"This doctrine of the divine mystery my mind embraced with joy, advancing towards God through the flesh, being called through faith to a new birth and endowed with a power for the attainment of a

[1] This looks as if Hilary had known, in St. John i. 18, the reading "The only-begotten God," instead of "The only-begotten Son." The revisers of 1881 testify to its antiquity.

heavenly regeneration; recognising the care of its Parent and Creator towards it, and convinced that it would not be reduced to nothingness by Him Who had called out of nothingness into its present state of existence."

Hilary accepted the doctrine concerning the divine attributes and the Incarnation, not as discoverable by natural reason, but as attained by the boundlessness of faith. But he evidently thought them not to be opposed to reason, for his understanding could, in some measure, understand them if only it believed. He dwells much on this, quoting freely from the Epistle of St. Paul to the Colossians (ii. 8–15), and then speaks of the probation for the world to come which is given in this life, in a brief section, headed with the words, " Faith in Christ removes both fear of death and weariness of life."

"In this repose, then, conscious of its own security, had my mind, rejoicing in its hopes, rested; and so far was it from fearing the interruption of death, as to regard it as the entrance into life eternal. But this life in the body it by no means regarded as miserable or painful to itself, but simply believed it to be what medicine is to the sick, swimming to the shipwrecked, learning to young men, military service to future commanders; that is to say, an endurance of the present state which should avail as preparation for the prize of a blessed immortality. Further, what it believed for itself, it also undertook to preach to others through the ministry of the priesthood laid upon it, extending the gift it had received into a work for the salvation of those around it."

The " De Trinitate " consists of twelve books. This number might have arisen out of the natural growth and progress of the treatise without any special design. But, if a reason for its choice were' to be sought, we might imagine that it had been suggested by the number of the months of the year, or of the tribes of Israel, or of the Apostles. Jerome, however, informs us that the ground of Hilary's choice lay in the fact that a classical writer, whom he greatly admired, the critic Quintilian, had divided into twelve books his treatise upon Oratory.

In the first book, as we have seen, Hilary maintains the reality of natural religion, and describes the manner in which its votaries are likely to be led onward to the acceptance of the revelation contained in the Holy Scriptures. The next four books discuss the baptismal *formula* recorded in the Gospel of St. Matthew (xxviii. 19); the union of the two natures in the One Person of Christ; and the testimony in favour of the Catholic faith on these subjects, which may be adduced from the writings of the prophets. The two following books (that is to say, the sixth and seventh) contain arguments, not only against the error of Sabellianism, on which we have already touched, but also on that of Manichæism.

Manichæism will come before us again in this little volume when we reach the case of Priscillian in connexion with the life of St. Martin. Its assertion of two independent principles, a good and an evil one, mutually opposing and thwarting each other, is not destitute of a certain plausibility.from some facts of nature. In the generation succeeding that of Hilary,

Manichæism found some very able defenders and expositors. How great a fascination it possesses for some minds is shown by the fact that it enchained for eight years the mighty intellect of St. Augustine.

The seventh book presents a feature not uncommon in ancient and in modern works of philosophy. Hilary maintains that the errors of the Ebionites (who taught that Christ was purely human), of the Arians (who made Him as nearly divine as a creature could possibly be), and of the Sabellians (who asserted a unity of personality as well as of substance in the Godhead), were mutually destructive of each other. Thus these errors, if rightly viewed, tended to confirm the convictions of true believers. " Their strife is our faith (*lis eorum est fides nostra*)," says Hilary. The eighth book is a demonstration of the unity of God. It shows that the eternal Sonship of Christ in nowise destroys that unity. The faith " does not take from the Son of God the position of the Only-begotten, but neither does it through that introduce a divinity of two Gods."

The remaining books of the " De Trinitate " are chiefly occupied with further refutations of Arianism, more especially in relation to single texts of the New Testament, which the Arians claimed as favourable to their doctrine. Throughout the treatise there are many admirable warnings, well worth the attention of readers in every generation, of the spirit in which Holy Scriptures should be studied. We subjoin two of these.

Here is our author's description of those who, as it were, patronise the faith rather than cherish it.

"There are many who, feigning faith, are not really subdued to the faith ; men puffed up by the breath of human emptiness, who establish a faith for themselves instead of truly accepting it."

Again : "He is the best reader who waits to gain from the words the sense of what is said instead of imposing a meaning on them, and who carries away their teaching instead of reading a doctrine into them."

A few more passages may serve to give a fuller notion of Hilary's general style. But at this point the reader may feel inclined to ask whether, beyond a generally able and devout treatment of his great theme, the author of the first extended treatise in the West has anything special to tell us, anything which has a bearing on theological questions of our own time. For if he only discourses in a pious and lofty vein concerning knowledge, which we may find set forth with still greater precision by opening our Prayer-books and reading carefully the three Creeds and the first five of the Thirty-nine Articles, then an acquaintance with Hilary's chief work may be elevating and improving, but can hardly be called suggestive, or, in the fullest sense, one that now tends to edification.

It must be answered, that on at least one point which has not yet been thought out, nor received all the attention which it deserves, Hilary's view is not only interesting and original, but has also a direct bearing upon the questions of our day.

That question is the following :—When we read in certain passages of Holy Scripture (as, for example, especially in St. Paul's Epistle to the Philippians, ii. 7), that the Son of God "emptied Himself," how

much does this imply in the way of acceptance on
the part of our Lord of the limitations of our human
ignorance ? That he condescended to learn, in a new
way, through the medium of those human powers
which for our sake He had adopted, truths which He
had known as God from all eternity, is a statement
generally accepted by theologians. But did He,
whose personality resides in His divinity, place, as
it were, in abeyance during his sojourn on earth any
portion of that power and knowledge which He had
ever enjoyed in Heaven ? It is perhaps hardly too
much to say that orthodox writers, who claim our
respect from learning and character, give somewhat
different answers to this question.

Now, Hilary certainly suggests an answer. He
considers that " the taking the form of a servant "
involved the consequence that the Incarnation was
not from the beginning complete—that is to say, that
as the form of the Godhead belongs to Christ's divinity, and He divested Himself of this form during
His earthly life, He did not, until His exaltation, join
to our human nature the complete essence of the
Godhead. Not that there was in Christ at any
moment any cessation of His divine existence. That
could not be. He remained always God, and capable
at any moment of resuming His true form. But of
His own free will, according to Hilary, He from
time to time subjected Himself from the day of His
Incarnation to that of His resurrection to those
weaknesses of suffering and of ignorance to which
humanity is liable. When, however, He displayed
acts of power, and when He uttered words of divine

wisdom; He was resuming and reasserting the action proper to His full and perfect Godhead.[1]

As, however, we are able to refer our readers elsewhere for further illustrations of what is most peculiar to Hilary, but at the same time most difficult, we prefer to set forth a few practical passages which have not hitherto been rendered into English, nor, we believe, into any modern language.

Some extracts from the second book of the " De Trinitate " will serve to show how keenly Hilary felt that these discussions were undesirable in themselves, but rendered necessary by the restlessness of heresy.

" It used to be enough for believers to receive that word of God which by the testimony of the Evangelist was poured into our ears with the actual power of its own truth, how the Lord says, ' Go ye into all nations, baptising them in the name of the Father, the Son, and the Holy Ghost ; teaching them to observe all things whatsoever I command you ; and lo, I am with you always even unto the end of the

---

[1] The reader who desires to enter more fully into these mysterious questions will find a full and sympathetic account of Hilary's view in the great work of Dorner on "The Person of Christ." But for an admirably-compressed statement of the case he is referred to the chapter headed, " St. Hilary on the Divine Sonship," in a volume on "The Church in Roman Gaul," by Canon Travers Smith ("Home Library," S. P. C. K.). In the above paragraphs the writer is at least as much indebted to Canon Smith as to Dorner. These two critics put a favourable interpretation on Hilary's language concerning the relation of our Lord's human nature to the Virgin Mother. They seem to think that Hilary only meant to press a principle generally admitted by the Fathers, namely, that the Son took his human body through the soul.

world.' For what is there that is not therein contained concerning the mystery of the salvation of
mankind?[1] Or what is there that is defective or
obscure? For all the words are full, as coming from
Him who is full; and perfect, as coming from Him
who is perfect. . . . . But we are compelled by
the faults of heretics and blasphemers to do what
would otherwise be unlawful, to climb up lofty
heights, to speak on matters beyond the powers of
human expression, to presume, where full knowledge
has not been vouchsafed to us. And whereas the
divine precepts ought to be fulfilled by faith alone—
namely, the adoration of the Father, the veneration
of the Son, the abounding in the gifts of the Holy
Ghost, we find ourselves compelled to extend our
humble powers of discourse into regions where language fails, and we are forcibly driven into a faulty
province of thought by reason of the faults of others.
Themes, which should have remained free from discussion because of our reverent scruples, are thus
forced forward into the perilous sphere of human
speech. For many have arisen who interpret the
simplicity of heavenly words in accordance with a
sense imposed on them by their own will, not that
which the actual force of what is said demands."

Hilary mentions by name, though only in a passing
way, some Gnostic sectarians, and (a little more in

[1] Literally, "concerning the sacrament of human salvation."
The early Fathers, as Keble and others have remarked, use the
term sacrament in a very extended sense; applying it to any of
the Christian mysteries, and to events and ordinances which
may be regarded as types and figures of those mysteries.

detail) the error of Sabellius, already noticed by us, and of the Ebionites, who represented the Redeemer as a mere man, though miraculously born of the Virgin Mary. He then declares his own anxiety, and the reluctance with which he undertakes the task of attempting to explain things truly :—

"Assuredly, to me, when I attempt to reply to these men, there arises, as it were, a seething tide of cares. There is the risk of slipping as regards the sense, there is the feeling of stupefaction in the province of the intellect ; and one must confess, not merely that language is infirm, but that one's very speech is silence. In truth, the actual will to make the attempt is extorted from me, with the design of resisting the rashness of others, of meeting and confuting error, of providing instruction for the ignorant. . . . . The very nature of the subject devours the significance of words, the light that cannot be penetrated blinds the contemplation of sense, and that which passes all bounds exceeds the capacity of the understanding. But we, imploring the pardon of Him who is all these things, are about to dare to seek, to speak ; and—which is the only fitting pledge in so deep an investigation—we shall avow our belief in what has been revealed."

After speaking of the provision for the coming of Christ, Hilary expresses himself as follows on the Incarnation, surely not without much power and freshness :—

"Now in what follows we see the dispensation of the Father's will. The Virgin, the birth, the body ; and subsequently the cross, death, Hades, are our

I

salvation. For the sake of the human race was the
Son of God born of a Virgin, through the Holy Spirit,
Himself ministering to Himself in this operation;
and by His own, that is, God's, overshadowing might
implanting the germs of a body for Himself and
the beginnings of mortal flesh : so that being made
man he might receive into Himself from the Virgin
the nature of flesh, and that through the alliance of
this conjunction there might stand forth in Him a
sanctified body of the entire race ; that as all may be
built up in Him by the fact of His willing to take
bodily substance, so again He might be shed back
upon all through that in Him which is invisible.

"Therefore did the invisible image of God shrink
not from the shame of a human beginning, and
through conception, birth, the cradle, and infant
cries traverse the entire course of the reproach and
humiliations of our nature. What worthy return can
be made by us for the affection of so vast a conde-
scension?"[1]

Then, after a few eloquent lines on those seeming
contradictions between the infinite and finite natures
thus meeting in Christ, on which pious contemplation has ever loved to dwell, Hilary adds :—

"If any one shall cherish the idea that such things
are unworthy of God, let him be led to confess that
he himself is so much the more beholden to Him for
the benefit received, in proportion as all this seems
unbefitting to the divine Majesty. He, through

---

[1] The reader will remark how much Hilary's mind is saturated
with thoughts suggested by Holy Scripture. See, *e.g.*, Galatians
iv. 2 ; Hebrews ii. 14, 15, in connexion with these words.

whom man was created, needed not to·become man ; but we needed that God should become flesh and dwell among us, that by the taking to Himself the one flesh He might dwell in the innermost recesses of the flesh of the human race at large. His humiliation is the ennobling of us, His reproach becomes our honour; that He as God should abide in our flesh is in turn a renewal of us from fleshly nature into God."

We turn to our author's commentaries on Holy Scripture. It seems desirable, in a sketch of this kind, to confine our attention to such books of Hilary as are unquestioned. For this reason we shall pass by certain commentaries on the Pauline Epistles, and the fragments of a colloquy upon the book of Genesis, which has been lately put forth as the work of Hilary by the learned Benedictine, Dom Pitra.[1]

Hilary probably intended to have composed a commentary upon the Book of Psalms. But he either did not carry out this design, or else a large portion of the book has been lost. There are only extant his remarks on Psalms i., ii., ix.–xiii., li.–lxix., xci.–cl. Hilary was not a proficient in Hebrew learning. Such knowledge was rare among the Fathers of the ·first five centuries, Origen and St. Jerome being the only conspicuous exceptions. Hilary, like most of his contemporaries, was compelled to trust mainly to the famous Greek translation known as the *Septuagint.* He enjoyed,

[1] In the first of the interesting and valuable volumes, entitled *Spicilegium Solesmense* (Paris, 1852).

I 2

however, the advantage of the commentaries of the famous Alexandrian divine, Origen. His general line lies midway between that of critics who are solely engaged in urging the literal sense, and those who are exclusively intent upon the Christian application of the words to the Church and to its divine Head. It is right to notice that Hilary prayed God to give him a true understanding of His Holy Word, and that he returned thanks in a modest spirit for such light as had been vouchsafed to him. We give a few specimens of his treatment.

He explains to us how we are to understand Jerusalem in the Psalms.

" The Jerusalem which is in heaven, which is our mother, which is the city of the great King, of which I think those are now inhabitants who rose again at the time of our Lord's passion."

On Psalm cxix., part 16, " Mine eyes fail for Thy salvation, and for the words of Thy righteousness," Hilary writes :—

" The eyes fail when the sight, looking out eagerly for the fulfilment of some expectation, grows wearied. Now the Psalmist fixed the eyes of his soul on the salvation of God. What must be understood by the salvation we have frequently explained ; namely, that it is Jesus, who shall save His people from their sins. While others then filled their eyes with the desires of the world, and directed them towards the pleasures of the present life, the Psalmist fixed his on the salvation of God. Nor let us suppose that his eyes failed merely with the effort of contemplation. They do not rest only on the salvation of God, but also on the proclamation of His righteousness. [Such was Hilary's reading of verse 123 of Ps. cxix., *elogium justitiæ ejus*.] He confesses, then, the just proclamations of God. He knows that there are some, which, by the thoughtless and impious, are reckoned as unjust utterances : when the heart of Pharaoh is hardened to contumacy, ·and the obstinacy of an irreligious will is imputed to him ; when, of two nations yet unborn, it is told that the elder shall serve the younger ; and when, though neither has wrought any good, subservience is imposed on one, domination given to another ; when Adam is expelled from Paradise, that he may not eat of the Tree of Life. These things men, unable to enter into the idea of divine excellence, goodness, and justice, determine to be unjust, simply because *they* cannot understand them. But the eyes of the Psalmist fail in looking on the just utterances of this sort. For he knows that there is no injustice in these words of God, but that, at the advent of God our Saviour, these decisions are to be consummated, and will be perceived by us to have been works of justice."

Presently, on the words, " Deal with Thy servant according to Thy mercy " (cxix. 124) : —

" For there is need of His mercy that we may abide in the profession of our service. Weak is human infirmity in the way of gaining anything ; this is alone its natural duty to will, and to begin, to enrol itself into the family of God. It is the work of the divine mercy to help the willing, to strengthen the beginners, to welcome those who have come to Him. But we

must do what we can in the way of beginning, that He
may make perfect."

Hilary is certainly emphatic upon the side of our
position as free agents; more so, perhaps, than
Augustine would have altogether approved of.
Prayer, study of God's Word, fasting, preservation
of purity, are all to be employed, and through them
we are to place our hope on the mercy of · God,
which is, after all, the one great resource.   But our
fasts and alms must be undertaken in a right spirit,
and not casually.

"We (this is on Ps. cxix. part 19), if we fast once,
think that we have done enough; if we give anything
to a poor man out of the abundance of our private
property, we believe that we have fulfilled all righteousness; when, perhaps, our fasting has been done
to · please men, or to relieve a frame wearied with
feasting; and even during our fasts we meditate on
lawless passion, on wrongs ·to be done to others, on
hatreds; and our giving has arisen from our being
tired at the poor man's knock at the door, or from
our craving for a reputation for goodness in the vain
and idle judgment of men.   And then we think it
due to us that our petitions should be heard by God;
but the Psalmist hopes for all from God, looks for
everything from His mercy.   He fulfils, indeed, all
the works of goodness, but he does not think this
enough for salvation, unless he obtains mercy according to the compassions of God and His judgments."

We give one more specimen from a comment on
Ps. cxl. 6, "I said unto the Lord, Thou art my God."

"It is the mark of no light and scanty confidence to have said unto the Lord, *Thou art my God.* A mind given up to lust, to avarice, to self-pleasing, to drunkenness, cannot utter those words. All these things must we renounce, and put an end to our subservience to them and acquaintance with them, that by such renunciation we may dare to say, '*I have said unto the Lord, Thou art my God.*'"

Hilary proceeds to show that all true Christians are warranted in making these words their own, but that Christ could use them in a manner special and peculiar to Himself; and that He did virtually so employ them on many occasions, such as the multiplication of the loaves and fishes, at the raising of Lazarus, and at the acceptance of His cup of woe in the garden of Gethsemane.

It is curious to find the Saracens mentioned by a bishop of Gaul at so early a date. In the comment on Psalm cxx. 5 (on the words, "that I dwell in the tents of Kedar"), Hilary writes, "These are the men now called Saracens." The name became only too familiar to his countrymen between A.D. 1100–1270. It is also a curious coincidence that the famous victory of Charles Martel in A. D. 732 over the Saracens, which saved France and Europe from their domination, was won in the district between Poitiers and Tours, the episcopal seats of the two bishops whose careers we have attempted to elucidate in the limits of this humble volume.

The commentary on St. Matthew is the earliest in the Latin tongue on any one Gospel, just as the treatise on the Holy Trinity is also the first that was

published in the Western Church. We find it more
difficult to give specimens of this commentary than
of the reflections on the Psalms. Possibly, as a
rule, it seems less striking, or, perhaps, we look for
more on such a theme ; especially if we are at all
acquainted with the richness of an Augustine or a
Chrysostom, or of treatises formed out of a number
of authors, or with modern writings based upon
such.

Here is a passage on the Transfiguration :—

"But while He was yet speaking a bright cloud
overshadowed them, and they are encompassed with
the spirit of divine power. A voice from the cloud
proclaims that this is the Son, this the Beloved, this
He in Whom the Father is well pleased, this He Who
is to be listened to ; so that, after the condemnation
passed on Him by the world, the voluntary submission to the cross, He might be recognised as the
fitting author of true teaching, as having confirmed
by His own example the glory of the heavenly kingdom to be given to bodies after decease by the
resurrection from the dead. He roused His disciples
from their state of dread and alarm. Him they see
alone Whom they had witnessed standing between
Moses and Elias. . . . He bids them preserve silence
respecting the events they had witnessed until He
should rise from the dead. For this was reserved as
a reward for their faith, that honour might be given
to disciples who had accepted, as in no wise light,
the authority of his precepts in themselves. Still He
had perceived that they were weak as yet for the
hearing of the voice. When they were filled with the

Holy Spirit, then should they be witnesses of spiritual events."

The following is his comment on the feeding of the Four Thousand (Matt. xv. 36, 37) :—

" The material supplied is thereupon increased, whether on the spots marked out as tables, or in the hands of the dispensers, or in the mouths of the eaters, I know not. By this deed the framer of the universe is made manifest."

In an earlier passage (xiv. 19) he refers to the holy Eucharist as "the heavenly food of eternal life."

The other works of Hilary will, in part at least, come under our notice in subsequent chapters. One of the most important, in his own day, was the one entitled "On Synods" ("De Synodis"). It was a letter written by the Bishop of Poitiers during his exile in Phrygia to his brother bishops in Gaul. It was what we should now call an *Irenicon*, beseeching all possible gentleness of consideration for the Semi-Arians, and putting the best construction that could be allowed upon their phraseology while appealing to them ; at any rate, not to deny the lawfulness of the term " of one substance " (*homöousion*) even if they were not yet prepared to accept it. In adopting this course Hilary was (though it would seem independently) taking the same line as his great compeer, Athanasius. But there were not wanting those who thought that Hilary had conceded too much. Their opinions found a spokesman in a brave, outspoken, but some-what harsh-minded, defender of the faith, Lucifer, bishop of Cagliari. A rejoinder to Lucifer by Hilary

was printed for the first time by the Benedictines in
their edition of Hilary's work in 1693. It is couched
in terms of great courtesy. But this treatise demands
a chapter to itself.

Very different in tone is Hilary's book against
Auxentius, bishop of Milan. But, then, Auxentius
really seems to have been a double-minded man,
who pretended to be orthodox, but was really an
Arian at heart. It was written in A.D. 365, and will
be brought before the reader as we proceed.

Some further notice must be taken of a lost
historical work which Hilary composed between the
years 360 and 366. Written against two Arian
bishops, Valens and Ursacius, it contained a history
of the Councils of Rimini and Seleucia. The fragments, first published in 1598, are of considerable
value, and have been only employed by modern
historians of the Church, as, for example, Canons
Robertson and Bright. But the suspicion, to say the
least, of early interpolations necessarily lessens the
authority of the collection. The contest concerning
the documents contained in it is rendered all the
more keen, inasmuch as, if the whole were accepted
as genuine, the case against Liberius, bishop of
Rome, would be much strengthened. That some of
the fragments do not deserve our confidence must,
we think, be conceded by unbiassed disputants.

During his exile in Phrygia, Hilary learnt, either
directly or indirectly, that there was some prospect of
his daughter, Abra, being sought in marriage, though
she was only in her thirteenth year. Hilary wrote a
letter, drawing a picture, in somewhat mystic language,

of the heavenly bridegroom, and with it he sent a morning and an evening hymn. The letter evidently hints that the bishop would prefer hearing that his daughter had resolved to embrace a life of celibacy. But he desires her to use her own judgment, and on any difficulty in the letter or in the hymns Abra is to consult her mother.[1]

Some readers may possibly look for the expression of opinion on the question whether the life and writings of St. Hilary have any very direct and important bearing upon the points at issue between ourselves and our Roman Catholic fellow-Christians. The answer must probably be in the negative, if direct evidence be sought for. So far as indirect evidence is concerned, it seems to the present writer (though this will be put down perhaps to Anglican prejudice) that what is to be found is, in almost every case, hostile to the claims of Rome. Let us glance at four points: development; the honour to be accorded to the Virgin Mother of the Lord; the position of the Bishop of Rome; and the general question of authority.

1. Undoubtedly the works of Hilary do suggest the existence of a doctrine of development. Such a doctrine is implied also in the writings of the historian Evagrius in the fifth century, and, again, very frequently in the writings of St. Augustine. But it need

---

[1] It is right to say that some eminent men, as Erasmus and Cave, do not consider this letter genuine. The present writer is unconvinced by their arguments. Hilary would naturally address a young girl, his own daughter, in a style differing from that adopted to bishops and emperors.

not involve more than this—that, to use the words of Augustine, "many things pertaining to the Catholic faith, while in course of agitation by the hot restlessness of heretics, are, with a view to defence against them, weighed more carefully, understood more clearly, and preached more earnestly ; and the question mooted by the adversary hath become an occasion of our learning." Thus much was always granted by the late Professor Hussey, of Oxford, in criticising the theory of Cardinal Newman and his allies. But it had been preached before the same university by Dean Hook many years earlier—before the rise of controversy upon the subject.

2. As regards the honour to be given to her whom all generations shall call blessed, the language of our author seems at times to fall short of that employed by great Anglican divines such as Bishop Pearson, Bishop Bull, and many more. Even in the strongest passage which virtually concedes the title of *Theotokos*, or God-bearer, which is so thoroughly recognised by the Anglican doctors, Hilary speaks of the Virgin as having to endure the severity of God's judgment at the Last Day.

3. Hilary had certainly an exalted opinion of the position of St. Peter as spokesman and leader of the Apostolic College. But this of itself proves nothing. In the works of St. Cyprian, of Bishop Pearson,[1] we find a similar recognition, but unless it is further conceded that the Bishop of Rome is successor to

---

[1] Compare "The Genesis of the Church," by Dr. Cotterill, bishop of Edinburgh (Blackwood, 1872), especially part i., chap. iv.

the powers of St. Peter, in a sense which is untrue of other bishops, nothing is proved.

4. The truth seems to be that Hilary conceded authority to conscience, to Holy Scripture, to Church councils, without ever putting forth any theory of the precise weight to be accorded to each element. How he was himself led on by conscience and right reason is clear from the first extract given in this chapter. As regards Holy Scripture, it must suffice in this place to point to the same passage, and to Hilary's assertion that he had learnt the doctrine contained in the Nicene Creed from the New Testament, though he had never heard the creed itself until he was on the point of exile. At a later date he seems to countenance the statement in Newman's "Arians" that too many of the bishops who had been present at Nicæa did not stand up boldly for the faith on their return to their dioceses; and that its preservation was, in many cases, mainly due to the courage and fidelity of the Christian laity. .

In his journey into North Italy, and his travels in those parts with Eusebius of Vercelli, there is not a word of any permission being asked of the Bishop of Rome. Indeed, some of the strongest evidence respecting the fall of the Roman Pontiff, Liberius (who, for a time, gave some degree of countenance to Arianism), is derived from a collection of letters originally made by Hilary, though subsequently it would seem interpolated. In the words of a living Roman Catholic historian, the Duc de Broglie, "it seems impossible to destroy the concurrence of testimonies which attest the fall of Liberius; but we admit that it is very difficult to determine the extent and the character of his false step." But a more detailed examination of this subject must be reserved for a later chapter.

On the whole, Hilary seems to write and to act in the spirit of the often-quoted saying of St. Cyprian, to the effect that "the episcopate is one of which each bishop possessses an unlimited liability." A bishop evidently supporting heresy, in Hilary's judgment, lost his rights, and the Bishop of Poitiers was prepared to wield the influence conferred on him not only by his ecclesiastical rank, but his character for courage and ability in defence of the Catholic faith, wherever it might be assailed. This view of Hilary's position and career is, at any rate, not inspired by any of those insular prepossessions of which British writers are often accused. It struck the eminent Roman Catholic divine, Möhler, who, as we have already remarked, has justly applied to Hilary the words used by Gibbon concerning the contemporary work of Athanasius that, " in a time of public danger, the dull claims of age and rank are sometimes superseded."

That we may not, however, close this chapter with merely controversial thoughts, we subjoin a few more extracts from Hilary's greatest work, the " De Trinitate," which must commend themselves, we would fain hope, to every Christian mind.

"It is perfect knowledge so to know God, that thou shouldst know Him to be not indeed one who is shrouded from our knowledge, but one whose nature we cannot worthily express. We must believe in Him, recognise Him, adore Him, and by such duties ought we to express what He is."—Bk. ii., chap. vii.

Again :—

" God, in His love for the world, exhibited this proof of His love, the giving of His only-begotten Son. If the proof of His love had consisted only in setting forth a creature for creatures ; giving for the world that which was of the world ; and redeeming beings sprung from nothing by a being sprung from nothing like themselves ; a sacrifice thus weak and unimportant would not call forth a faith of great worth. But precious is that which evidences love ; and greatness is measured by what is great. God, in His love for the world, gave not an adopted Son, but His own, the only-begotten. In Him is the real property of the Father, nativity and truth, no mere creation, nor adoption, nor semblance. The pledge of God's love and charity is to have given for the salvation of the world His own and only-begotten Son."

CHAPTER XIII.

HILARY'S "IRENICON."

ALTHOUGH in a previous chapter we have given a slight general idea of the circumstances which induced Hilary to compose[1] his treatise on the Synods, yet the importance of the book demands, even at the risk of a slight repetition, some further notice, and that more lively idea of its character and tone which will, we trust, be supplied by the translation of some portion of its contents. The full title of this letter runs as follows :—"On the Synods of the Catholic Faith against the Arians, and against Perverters of the Faith who take the side of the Arians."

The address of this treatise presents a rather difficult study in what may be termed the ecclesiastical geography of the time, that is to say, at the close of A.D. 358, or the commencement of the year following. Literally translated, it runs thus :—

"To my most beloved and blessed brethren and fellow-bishops of the provinces of the first and second Germany, the first and second Belgica, the first and second Lyonesse, of the province of Aquitania, and the province of the Nine-Nations, of the Narbonian province, especially the people and clergy of Toulouse, and to the bishops of the British provinces,

---

[1] Chapter ix., "Hilary and the Semi-Arians," pp. 56, 57.

Hilary, the servant of Christ, wishes eternal salvation in God and our Lord."

It would probably be impossible, and hardly worth while even if possible, to trace the precise bounds of the various provinces here named. But commentators have succeeded in discovering, in most instances, the name of the ecclesiastical metropolis of each; and this knowledge gives a very fair general notion of the people whom the Bishop of Poitiers was addressing. These head-quarters of Church authority stood as follows (for convenience sake we give the modern names) :—For the first Germany, Mainz (or Mayence) ; for the second Germany, Köln (Cologne); for the first Belgica, Trier (Trèves) ; for the second Belgica, Rheims ; for the first Lyonesse, Lyons ; for the second Lyonesse, Rouen ; for the province of the Nine-Nations (roughly corresponding with Gascony) a town near the present site of Agen. The special mention of Toulouse probably arises from the circumstance that its bishop, by name Rhodanius, had been kept firm in the faith, though of a yielding nature, by the influence of Hilary,[1] and was at this time involved in the same sentence of exile. As regards the last in this list, the *provinciarum Britan- nicarum episcopi*, it must be observed that they are bishops long antecedent to the mission of St. Augustine and the establishment of *Dorobernium* or Kent- town (for such is the meaning of *Cantuaria*), now known to us as Canterbury, as the seat of the primacy.

---

[1] We learn this, not from Hilary himself, but from Sulpicius Severus, the author of two books on Church History, as well as of the " Life of St. Martin."

K

For Hilary is writing, at the latest, in A.D. 359, whereas the date of St. Augustine's mission is A.D. 597.

Hilary begins by explaining that he had for some time thought silence best. But he understands that the rarity of communication on the part of his brethren in Gaul has arisen from the distance caused by his exile, and the actual ignorance on the part of many of the country to which he was banished. But he now hears, to his delight, that for three years his brother-bishops have refused communion to Saturninus; are thoroughly at heart with him who now addresses them ; and have not only declined to accept, but have condemned, the formula drawn up by an assembly held at Sirmium. Hilary proceeds thus :—

"I have now felt it to be a duty and an act of piety to transmit, as a bishop to bishops who hold communion with me in Christ, the conversation of salutary and faithful discourse ; so that I, who in my fear of uncertain issues was congratulating myself on my personal freedom from all these difficulties, might now rejoice in the integrity of our common faith. O unshaken firmness of your noble conscientiousness ! O strong house built on the foundation of the faithful rock.[1] O uninjured and undisturbed constancy of an inviolate will ! "

Hilary assures his friends that the news of the

---

[1] The Benedictine editor, Dom Coutant, justly remarks that Hilary here seems to allude to the *confession* of St. Peter, that Jesus was "the Christ, the son of the living God," as the rock. He twice asserts this in the "De Trinitate" (ii. 23, vi. 36), which was prior to his "De Synodis" in point of date.

firmness and decision of their faith has, even at this
late hour, produced considerable effect upon the
temper and conduct of some Oriental prelates, who
had given way to the decrees promulgated at Sirmium.
He now writes, however, not merely to congratulate
them on their behaviour and its good results, but also
to answer the inquiries addressed to him by some
among them as to the positions taken up by the
Orientals. The task thus imposed upon him is a
difficult one; for, if it is hard to put into words one's
own belief, it is still harder to set forth the belief
entertained by others. He will try his best. Only
let them be sure to read his epistle to the end, and
not to judge him until that is done. In that case
he is not without hope that crafty heretics may fail
in their attempts to deceive, and that the sincere
upholders of the Catholic faith may attain what they
so much desire. Hilary then describes those mutual
suspicions of the Oriental and Gallican episcopate,
to which reference has been made in a former chapter ;
how the language of the Westerns seemed to their
brethren in the East to be tinged with Sabellianism,
while in turn the bishops in Gaul supposed their
fellow-prelates in Asia to be in danger of lapsing into
thorough Arianism.

It is necessary, in the first place, then, for Hilary
to show forth with all possible definiteness (*ut verbis
quàm possim absolutissimis demonstrem*), the precise
tenour of the protests made by the Orientals against
the decrees of the Council of Sirmium (the one known
as the Second Sirmian, held in A.D. 357); "not," he
says, "that all this was not most clearly published by

others, but because an exact verbal translation from Greek into Latin generally causes obscurity. Since the care taken to preserve a parallelism between the actual words employed cannot succeed in creating the same definite impression upon ordinary understandings."

Let it be permitted to us to remark, in passing, that this is a problem of all time, and not confined to translations from Greek into Latin. The Venerable Bede refers to the same difficulty when he attempts to give a Latin version of a hymn of the earliest Anglo-Saxon poet, Cædmon; and a great master of language in our own day, John Henry Newman, has also dwelt upon it in two of his Anglican works. To find it, however, acknowledged by Hilary is peculiarly gratifying to one who, like the present writer, is among the first, he believes, who have attempted to present certain portions of Hilary's own writings in an English dress.[1]   Hilary could not complain if he found that an English version of his own writings occasionally became a paraphrase.

It is curious to find Hilary in some degree anticipating the criticism of Erasmus upon the question of ignorance, and evidently intimating that to pretend ignorance concerning that which has been clearly revealed amounts to an abnegation of duty. Among the sadder elements of the story told in the " De

---

[1] One or two of Hilary's hymns have been translated ; and there is an excellent version (from which many good hints have been obtained) of Hilary's account of his own conversion by the Rev. W. S. Grignon, in an appendix to the very valuable Bampton Lectures of Professor Wace, for 1879.

Synodis," is that of the ambiguous Creed of Sirmium
being signed by Hosius of Cordova, who had been
one of the leading bishops on the orthodox side at
Nice, possibly the actual president of that famous
council. Hilary, however, does not appear to have
been aware of some mitigating circumstances. The
creed, assigned in the "De Synodis" to the actual
penmanship of Hosius and another, was in all probability not actually composed by that prelate. It
may be said that this is a fact of minor importance,
if, after all, Hosius set his signature to this fallacious
document. But we learn from other sources that he
was more than a hundred years old when he thus
acted, and, further, that it was under the pressure of
torture.[1]

Hilary criticises this document (known as the
Creed of Sirmium) with great ability, showing on the
one hand where it falls short of the full truth, and on
the other what large admissions heretics were now
willing to make, as feeling the pressure of Scriptural authority (*conclusi Scripturarum auctoritatibus*).
Having already pointed out the weakness and inconsistency of the Semi-Arian creed, we need not here
dwell upon our author's analysis of it. Hilary passes
on to an account of a synod held at Antioch. This
was a synod of high repute held in A.D. 341, on the
occasion of the dedication of a church of which

---

[1] Socrates, "Hist. Ecclesiast.," lib. ii., cap. 31 ; Sozomen,
" Hist. Ecclesiast.," lib. iv., cap. 6, 12. Sulpicius Severus,
"Sacr. Hist.," lib. ii., appeals to a letter of Hilary to the
effect that Hosius was more than a centenarian at this time.
But this letter, with many of Hilary's, has been lost.

Constantine himself had laid the foundations.[1] The main object before the ninety bishops who composed it was to condemn, not Arianism, but the Sabellianism which had sprung up since the date of the great gathering at Nicæa. It was at this point that there came in some of the difficulties of translation to which reference has been made. The Greek-speaking Fathers spoke of "three *hypostases* in one *ousia*," which Hilary translates "three *substances* in one *essence*"; though he evidently meant what was afterwards better expressed as "three persons in one essence." Even here, however, we must carefully bear in mind that the term *person* is not to be understood as meaning all that it implies in human agents —namely, an independent unity.[2]

Accounts of other synods and documents follow. Then comes a summary of the difficulties which have arisen, partly from the profound nature of the questions at issue, and partly from the lamentable ignorance even of those who ought to have been guides and teachers of the flock.

"So great is the peril of the Eastern Churches, that it is rare to find either priests or people sound in the faith. Sadly through the fault of some has authority been granted to impiety; and in consequence of the banishment of bishops, whose case is

---

[1] Athanasius, in his treatise "On Synods," and the historians, Socrates (lib. ii., cap. 8), and Sozomen (lib. iii., cap. 5), give an account of it. Constantius was present.

[2] The difficulty of language has been fully explained in the later editions of Newman's "Arians," chap. ii., sec. ii. of Appendix iv.

not unknown to you, the strength of the profane ones has been increased." And here comes in that sad account of the spiritual condition of Asia Minor which has been already quoted in our eighth chapter —that on "Hilary and the Semi-Arians."

Hilary then proceeds to admit that the objection to the term "of one substance" (*homöousion*), on the ground that it may, under certain circumstances, be supposed to suggest Sabellianism, has not been wholly unreasonable. It needs to be set forth in such a context and such a manner as may render its ortho-doxy clear and unmistakable.

"Let us urge no solitary phrase from among the divine mysteries in such wise as to cause suspicion on the part of hearers and give occasion to the blasphemer. *The one substance* may be uttered with piety, may be kept in silence with piety."

Hilary then proceeds, while criticising the danger of the worst sense being attached to it, to admit that the Semi-Arian watchword "of like substance" (*homoiousion*) may be patient of a good interpretation.

"I entreat you, brethren, remove suspicion, shut out occasions of offence. In order that the *homoiousion* may be approved, let us not find fault with the *homöousion*. Let us think of so many bishops, holy men and now at rest; what judgment will the Lord pass upon us if they are now anathematised by us ? . . . . For we were ordained by them, and we are their successors. Let us renounce the episcopate, because we shall have commenced its duties with an anathema. Make allowance, brethren, for my grief; the task on which you are venturing is an impious one. I cannot endure the suggestion, that any man avowing the *homöousion* in a religious sense should lie under an anathema. There is nothing criminal in a term which in nowise shocks the religious sense. I neither know nor understand the *homoiousion*, except as a confession of a like essence. I call to witness the God of heaven and earth, that I, when I had not yet heard either term, yet had always felt the lawfulness of each in such wise that by "*of one substance*" ought to be understood of like substance— that is, that nothing like to itself in nature could possibly exist, unless it were of the same nature. Baptised a considerable time since, and abiding for a short time in the episcopate, I never heard the Nicene Creed, except when on the point of exile; but the Gospels and the Epistles made clear to me the sense of the *homöousion* and *homoiousion*. Pious is the wish we cherish. Let us not condemn the Fathers, let us not give courage to the heretics, lest, while we drive heresy away, we nourish heresy. Our Fathers, after the Council of Nicæa, interpreted the fitness of the *one substance* in a religious spirit; their treatises are extant, full perception of what they meant abides with us; if anything in the way of addition is needed, let us consult about it in common. A most excellent condition of the faith may yet be built up amongst us, on the basis that nothing that has been well arranged may be disturbed, and all that is wrongly understood may be cut away.

"I have, O brethren beloved, gone beyond the modesty of human intelligence, and, forgetful of my humility, have written on matters so vast and recon-

dite, themes before this age of ours unattempted and
kept in silence, under the compulsion of my love for
you ; and I have told you my own belief, under the
conviction that I owe to the Church the service of
this my campaign, that by means of this letter I
should mark out distinctly the voice of my episcopate
in Christ in according with evangelic doctrine. It is
your duty so to treat in common, to provide, and so
to act, that what you abide in with faith inviolate up
to the present day you may preserve with religious
conscientiousness, and what you hold now you may
hold still. Be mindful in your holy prayers of my
exile. Pleasant as would be a return from that exile
to you in the Lord Jesus Christ, it is, I feel well-
nigh sure, after this my exposition of the faith, a
safer issue that I should die. That God and our
Lord may preserve you undefiled and uninjured
to the day of revelation is, brethren beloved, my
desire."

That this letter, conjoined as it was with consistent treatment of Semi-Arians throughout Hilary's
subsequent career, produced a great effect upon the
mind of Christian Gaul, can hardly be doubted. So
far as any hesitation arose concerning it, it was from
the orthodox, not from the Semi-Arian camp, that
it proceeded. There have been critics who have
regarded its concessions as somewhat exceeding those
which Hilary's great compeer, Athanasius, would
have been inclined to make. But Dom Coutant,
the Benedictine editor of the works of Hilary, appears
successfully to have disposed of this theory, alleging,
fairly enough, we think, that any slight seeming dis-

crepancy of tone may be accounted for by observation of the difference of dates and circumstances.
A conference between the defenders of the Nicene
Creed in the West and its still more remarkable
champion in the East would, in all human probability,
have proved that their line of action was virtually as
identical as the faith for which they were contending.
But, even if both were present, which is doubtful,
for a brief time at the Council of Seleucia in A.D.
359, the visit of Athanasius to that city was a secret
unknown, not merely to all his enemies but even
to most of his friends, so that the two allies never
met for conference. The period embraced in Hilary's
exile (which lasted, as we have said, for at least the
three years commencing with A.D. 356) is contemporary with the third expulsion of Athanasius from
Alexandria; the expulsion achieved in that same year
(356), by the secret orders of the dissembling Constantius, when, at the hour of midnight, Syrianus,
duke of Egypt, with five thousand soldiers, attacked,
with tumult and bloodshed, the congregation of
faithful worshippers gathered together in the church
of St. Theônas. That attack was the prelude to
similar outrages in the other churches of Alexandria,
which, for four months, remained, in the words of
Gibbon, "exposed to the insults of a licentious army,
stimulated by the ecclesiastics of a hostile faction."[1]

---

[1] "Decline and Fall," chap. xxi. This animated description is one of the many passages in Gibbon's great work which
ought to prevent sciolists in Church history from implying (as
they often do without openly affirming it) that the Arians were
always the persecuted party. Syrianus, we may observe, was

The insults and cruelties inflicted upon holy maidens, as well as upon bishops and presbyters, at the instigation of the Arians, need not here be told in detail.   The point with which we are here concerned is, that the main object of the assault, Athanasius himself, escaped into the desert, though not until he had seen the last of the congregation depart.   For six years (356–362) the Archbishop of Alexandria, in the inaccessible retreats of the deserts, lived as a monk among monks.   But, though constantly changing his place so as to elude pursuit, he continued to send forth his vigorous writings in defence of the faith and against Constantius.

In the romantic series of repeated exiles, in the concentration of all hostility against his individual self—insomuch that " Athanasius against the world " has passed into a proverb—in the imperial, though still humble and self-forgetting, care of all the churches, the place of the Bishop of Poitiers is undoubtedly below that of the great Archbishop of Alexandria. But the work of Athanasius would have remained far less thorough and complete, if, for the many thousands unacquainted with the Greek language, there had been no doctor in the West to teach, in

worthy of his master, Constantius.   He terrorised Alexandrians into signing documents to the effect that he had not used violence.   The original authorities, with documents, are given in the works of Athanasius ("Apologia de Fugâ," sec. 24 ; " Apologia ad Constantium," sec. 26 ; " Hist. Arian.," sec. 80). They are partly given also by Theodoret in his " Hist. Ecclesiast.," lib. ii., 14. Möhler's account agrees with Gibbon's, but, though adding some details, is, as a whole, less vivid and icturesque.

ways of his own and in the Latin, the great lessons
which his generation needed to learn.   Perhaps the
fact that they were never able to meet face to face
must be considered to enhance the substantial unity
of their creed and work.

Both found it necessary in some degree to break
with Lucifer of Cagliari. Athanasius, in a well-known
passage of his "De Synodis" (41), expressed his
willingness to regard as brethren those who accepted
all that was decreed at Nice, except the term "of
one substance." His most recent English biographer[1]
is, no doubt, right in insisting that Athanasius did not
consider that such a position on the part of the Semi-
Arians ought to be, or would be, a permanent one.
He was convinced that in time they would perceive
the value and importance of the term, and that it
would come to be accepted by them, as, in truth, it
has come to be accepted by Christendom at large ;
being, in the words of Gibbon, "unanimously received
as a fundamental article of the Christian faith, by the
consent of the Greek, the Latin, the Oriental, and
the Protestant Churches."

Hilary, in the work before us, evidently meant to
express similar sentiments. But Lucifer of Cagliari
thought that he had conceded too much, and had
recognised the Semi-Arians as being now ih full
possession of the truth. In a kindly and courteous
explanation sent to Lucifer, the Bishop of Poitiers
denied that he had meant or had said so much.

[1] Canon Bright, in his admirable and exhaustive article on
Athanasius in Smith and Wace's "Dictionary of Ecclesiastical
Biography."

"I said not they had proffered the true faith, but a hope of recalling the true faith."

A few years later, the submission of opponents of the Creed of Nicæa was made upon so large a scale that the question of the terms on which they were to be received was anxiously debated. Reconciliations of this nature are proverbially matters of much delicacy. The discussion on the terms to be granted to those who had lapsed had, in a previous generation, caused long and bitter controversy, and had largely contributed to the schismatic movement known as Novatianism. Happily no such serious rent arose out of the negotiations between the orthodox and the returning Arians or Semi-Arians. Nevertheless, the Bishop of Cagliari, unable to accept the gentle terms offered by the majority, refused to communicate not only with those who had been misled at Rimini, but also with all who had received such even when they had manifested their repentance. A few, hence called *Luciferians*, sided with him. The general feeling branded them as schismatics ; and Jerome, though partially excusing the leader, wrote a treatise against his followers. Some who did not agree with Lucifer yet shrunk from positive condemnation. The Church historian, Sulpicius Severus, who will subsequently come before us as the biographer of St. Martin, declines to pronounce a judgment on the case. But if he hesitates here (on the whole, we venture to think, mistakenly), on one point he feels no doubt whatever. " This," writes Sulpicius, " is admitted on all hands, that our Gaul was freed from the guilt of heresy by the good work of Hilary alone."

CHAPTER XIV.

HILARY AS HISTORIAN.

THE activity of our prelate's mind was not sufficiently occupied by the production of Commentaries on Holy Scripture and dogmatic theology, by letters to Constantius, or to his friends in Gaul. In addition to these labours, Hilary, as we have already observed, composed between A.D. 360–366 an historic work, in which he intended to give some account of the Coun cils of Seleucia and Rimini, and to explain how it came to pass that the Council of Rimini, summoned by Constantius, was led to oppose the orthodox Creed of Nicæa.

Of this history we only possess fragments, and, most unfortunately, these fragments are not in a sound condition. At an early period, seemingly while Hilary was yet alive, some interpolations crept into the work; and this circumstance throws a shadow of doubtfulness over the value of the fragments, considered as a whole. Many statements, however, contained in them receive abundant corroboration from independent sources, and, in turn, throw light upon incidents narrated by other authors. Such are, for example, the calumnious charge against the great Athanasius, that he had slain a man named Arsenius, who was subsequently produced alive; the equally calumnious, though less grave, accusation against one of the deacons of Athanasius,—Macharius,—that he had broken a chalice ; the mention of a letter from the Egyptian bishops to their brother prelate, Julius, bishop of Rome, and the like. These, with many more details of a like kind, are testified to by Theodôret and also by St. Athanasius himself.

The same must be said concerning a summary of the many brutalities enacted against orthodox prelates, and even holy maidens, by Arians, which forms part of a narrative of the Council of Sardica. That council, summoned by Constantius and Constans, met at some period not earlier than A.D. 343, nor later than 347,—the precise date is much disputed,—at this town in Illyricum. Its site coincides, or nearly coincides, with that of the modern town of Sophia. There were present about seventy-six Eastern and a hundred Western bishops; and Hosius, of Cordova, who had probably been president at Nice, again occupied the same honourable position. Whether from the stress of business, from its being imprudent to quit Rome, or (as Dean Milman suggests) a dislike to risk the growing dignity of his see by provoking comparison with the Bishop of Cordova, Julius, the bishop of Rome, did not attend. He sent, however, two, or possibly even three, episcopal legates to represent him.

How far Hilary would have shone as an historian, in what degree his narrative would have strengthened his case against the two Arian bishops of Gaul— Valens and Ursacius—for whose confutation he composed it, we have no sufficient means of judging.

In the shape in which it has come down to us, it rather resembles a collection of materials for history (*mémoires pour servir à l'histoire*, as our neighbours call them), than a history properly so called. Nevertheless, these fragments are far from valueless, and events of the last twenty years have somewhat enhanced the interest felt concerning them.

It is not immediately obvious why our author interwove into his history an event so far back as the Council of Sardica. The mention of a local council, summoned at Arles in A.D. 353, is intelligible enough. For not only was this council held in Gaul, but it brought to the front the man who was to prove Hilary's chief opponent, Saturninus. This prelate, with his Arian allies, succeeded in obtaining from this council a decree of banishment against the devout and orthodox Paulinus, bishop of Trèves. Hilary shows that the point then at issue was a question of faith, and no mere opinion concerning the conduct of an individual prelate ; in other words, that it turned upon the Creed of Nicæa, not upon the question whether the conduct of Athanasius should be condemned. This is the subject of the first of these historic fragments.

To go back after this commencement upon the Council of Sardica looks like a faulty arrangement, which may, perhaps, have arisen from the disorganised state in which the book has come down to us. However, it gives Hilary an opportunity of not only defending the course pursued by Athanasius, but of confirming his defence by the evidence of the two prelates against whom, as we have said, the book is written— Valens and Ursacius. The career of these two bishops, though far less violent than that of Saturninus, had been extremely wavering and inconsistent.

In two letters (one addressed to Julius, bishop of Rome, the other to Athanasius himself) they had recognised the innocence of that great champion of truth, and pronounced the various charges against him to be false. But at a council held at Sirmium in 349, and subsequently at Milan, these acquittals were reversed; and the above-named Gallican prelates appear to have been among those who changed sides.

The same difficulty had nearly broken up the Council of Sardica. Athanasius, with his two companions, Marcellus of Ancyra, and Asclepas, claimed the right to sit and vote, but Eusebius of Nicomedia and his partisans would not allow this without a fresh trial. When the Eusebians could not carry their point, they fled, and organised a rival council at the neighbouring city of Philippopolis.

The Council of Sardica has not been deemed of a sufficiently important and representative character to rank among those which are commonly called ecumenical. It is true that one or two great names among Roman Catholic writers may be cited on behalf of its ecumenicity, and that here and there we may find it so called in controversial works written by Ultramontanes. But few, if any, Roman Catholic writers of repute would now venture to claim such a position for it. M. de Broglie disclaims it, and so does even Hefele.

The last-named author not only shows that the weight of authority during the last 300 years is against

L

its ecumenicity, but that conclusive arguments from patristic testimony can be adduced. St. Gregory the Great and St. Isidore of Seville only knew of *four* general councils—the famous ones of Nice and Constantinople, of Ephesus and Chalcedon. St. Augustine, though he had heard of the Eusebian gathering (which called itself a Council of Sardica, even after its removal to Philippopolis), was entirely ignorant of the fact that an orthodox synod had been held at Sardica. Now, this is inconceivable, if it had been acknowledged as an ecumenical council.

Once again we may seem to be wandering far away from the words and deeds of Hilary of Poitiers. The link of connexion will, however, soon become discernible. The Council of Sardica is one of those assemblages which, though not in the first rank, yet did aid in producing results of importance. It certainly gave an impulse to the growing power of the see of Rome. For its third and fourth canons allow a bishop deposed by his comprovincial bishops, or non-suited in a case of importance, to appeal to the Bishop of Rome, so that he might obtain a re-hearing of his case ; not, indeed, directly by the Bishop of Rome, but by judges of neighbouring provinces appointed by that bishop.

Moreover, in the third canon we find the following words introduced :—" If it seem good to you, let us honour the memory of the blessed Apostle Peter, and let letters be addressed to [Julius] the bishop of Rome by those who have been the judges ; and let him, if it seem fitting, reopen the case." The seventh canon runs somewhat similarly. Now, although these canons do not appear in the "Fragmenta" of Hilary, we do find therein a letter from the Sardican bishops to Julius allowing that he had good reason for not being present in person at the synod, and "that it was best and fittest that the bishops from all the provinces should make their reports to the head—that is, the chair of St. Peter."

Over the canons of Sardica a fierce contest has been waged between the great and learned school of Gallican divines, such as De Marca, Dupin, with several others, and the Roman Ultramontanes, or (as Hefele calls them), Curialists. The Gallicans, while pointing out the limitations of the cases, yet maintain that these canons involved a novelty; and they seem to imply that, as coming from a council not recognised as ecumenical, they sanction something like an usurpation. The Curialists not only strain them beyond their natural meaning, but declare that, far from being a novelty, these canons only state formally what was already recognised informally, and (as English jurisprudents would phrase it), at the most, convert common law into statute law. Yet even such a change may prove very potent, for it forms a secure basis for further aggression.

Distinguished modern divines, who are far removed from any sympathy with distinctively Roman Catholic doctrine, admit that the providence of God, in this instance, as in so many more, over-ruled to good much that was abstractedly indefensible. They also grant that natural causes, such as the imperial character of the capital of Italy, combined with some of the merits of the early occupants of the see,[1] produced that excessive domination which by the fourteenth century had become too great for any mere mortal, even with the best intentions, to be able to wield it aright. Thus, to take one example out of many, the late Professor Hussey of Oxford, in a succinct and able essay *against* the Roman Supremacy, when treating of the age of Hilary and Athanasius, writes as follows:—"Rome at that time, and for some time afterwards, had earned the precedence in honour always allowed to the imperial see, not only by her martyred bishops and her munificence to poorer Churches, but also by her orthodoxy, and by the courage and ability with which she undertook the championship of the truth against various shapes of error."

In attempting to form an opinion respecting the attitude of Hilary's mind towards the Roman claim, it must be owned that the evidence we have to proceed upon is somewhat scanty and imperfect. It is not even clear that he was acquainted with the actual canons passed at Sardica. The supposition that he was ignorant of their precise contents is certainly not more startling than is the fact that Augustine did not even know of the existence of an orthodox Council of Sardica. But, even if, which is more probable, Hilary was acquainted with them, it must be remembered that the majority of copies contain the word which we have placed in brackets ; that is to say, the name of Julius. The Sardican canons were published both

[1] Passages to this effect might be quoted from the works of Archbishop Trench, Bishop Harold Browne, the late Mr. Maurice, and many more.

in Latin and Greek ; and in the great work of Labbe on the *Concilia*, the name of the then Bishop of Rome appears both in the Greek copy and in one of the two Latin ones therein given.

It is no doubt possible—and a learned German Protestant, Spittler, strongly takes this view—that those who inserted the name of Julius may have done so without necessarily meaning to limit the powers therein assigned, so far as a non-ecumenical council could assign them, to the person thus named. Nevertheless, those who have seen even a little of the behind-scenes working of public bodies, alike in causes civil and ecclesiastical, must be aware how frequently the personal element affects the resolutions that nominally spring out of abstract considerations. Stated openly, they would constantly run somewhat as follows :—"Let such and such additional powers be conferred upon the prefect of such a city, for it is an ancient and central one ; and then, you know, the present prefect is such an excellent, genial, hospitable man." " Let such an extension of authority be refused to the bishop of such and such a diocese, because there would be found difficulties in the working out of the scheme ; and besides the present holder, A. B., with many good gifts, has incurred, whether justly or not, a prejudice in connexion with this or that event." True that in each case the first part is usually said aloud and the latter in a whisper ; but, for all that, it is often the whispered word that proves the more influential and the one which actually prevails.

Now Julius, who occupied the Roman see for

*

fifteen years (A.D. 337–352), had proved himself
through all these troublous times to be a model
prelate. He had maintained the truth of that great
central article of the Christian faith, the Incarnation,
which forms the chief glory of the human race ; and
he had loyally supported the action of its foremost
champion, Athanasius. Indeed, Rome, which until
the time of Leo I. made scarcely any direct contri-
bution to theology, had, under the sway of Julius,
not only welcomed the Bishop of Alexandria on the
occasion of his second exile from Egypt, but had
become (in Dean Milman's phrase) "the scholar as
well as the loyal partisan of Athanasius." Athanasius
impressed upon Latin Christianity the spirit of orthodoxy, and "introduced into Rome the knowledge
and practice of the monastic life."[1]

Consequently, a claim for an accession of authority
to "the bishop of the royal city,"[2] as Socrates calls
the Roman prelate, came before the Council of
Sardica with a great prestige in its favour. The
retirement of the Eusebians to Philippopolis left the
orthodox bishops in possession of the field. The
Council, sitting within the realms of the orthodox
Constans, reaffirmed the decisions of Nice, and compelled even Constantius to consent to a restoration
of Athanasius.

It would be interesting, if we possessed the entire
work of Hilary, to know how *he* understood the only
sentence contained in his extensive writings—and

[1] Gibbon. Compare Canon Bright's article, "Athanasius,"
in Smith and Wace's "Dictionary of Ecclesiastical Biography."
[2] "Hist. Eccles.," i., 8.

that sentence not his own—which even hints at a primacy residing in the Roman see. Did he regard what had been done as a power conferred simply on his friend Julius? Did he look at the Council of Sardica as in these matters a purely local one, and as solely conferring (whether on Julius or on his successors) a right of appeal from Illyricum and Macedonia? These provinces, though mainly Greek in race and language, formed part of the empire. That they should seek association with Rome in matters ecclesiastical as well as civil was only natural, more especially as the temporal authority in the East was at this time both heterodox and tyrannical; while at Rome both Church and State were on the side of orthodoxy.

To these questions we have no sufficient means of returning a satisfactory reply. Yet it does seem as if a certain course of action on the part of Hilary and certain portions of these "Fragments" may aid us in arriving at a conclusion which attains, to say the very least, to a high degree of probability.

The course of action has already been referred to, and must come under our notice once again. In his latest years, Hilary resolved to leave the home to which he had returned, and to confront, in his own quarters, the Arianising bishop of Milan, Auxentius. In this tour Hilary enjoyed the company and aid of Eusebius, bishop of Vercelli. It seems to have been injured by the opposition of Lucifer of Cagliari. It was brought to a termination by the stern mandates of the emperor, Constantius. But, as we have already observed, not one single hint can be discovered of

the slightest appeal to the authority of the Bishop of
Rome.

That bishop was the successor of Julius in the
Roman see, Liberius. That the conduct of Liberius
may have greatly influenced the feeling of Hilary
towards the Roman see, is very possible. But, concerning that conduct, these " Fragments " are one of
the sources of evidence. Our general verdict, identical
with that of M. de Broglie, has already been given.
But at this point we must re-state the case a little
more in detail.

The question is whether Liberius, who became
bishop of Rome in A.D. 352, did or did not, during
any part of his career, lend countenance to the Arian
heresy.

There are large portions of Christendom, there are
large tracts of time in its history, when such a question
could only have been regarded as one of very subor-
dinate importance. It is impossible to describe such
a condition of feeling more clearly, or to state it
more emphatically, than has been done by the greatest
doctor of the Western Church, St. Augustine. Writing
against Donatist adversaries, he exclaims, " It is a
consolation by no means slight, nay, of no mean
glory, to be criminally accused, in company with the
Church itself, by the enemies of the Church ; yet her
defence does not depend on the defence of those
men whom they [the Donatists] attack with their
false charges. Assuredly, whatever may have been
Marcellinus, Marcellus, Silvester, Melchiades [bishops
of Rome], Mensurius, Cæcilianus [bishops of Car-
thage], *no damage accrues to the Catholic Church*

diffused throughout the universe, in no wise are we
crowned by their innocence, in no wise are we condemned by their iniquity."[1]

Christendom at large would still be prepared to
re-echo these trenchant and decided accents, so long
as the terms *innocence* or *iniquity* referred to moral
conduct only. But the work of Augustine in which
they occur touches upon questions concerning doctrine
even more than on those connected with morality.
In the matter now to be discussed—the case of
Liberius—the case is essentially doctrinal.

To begin with what is admitted on all sides. The
commencement of the episcopate of Liberius was
marked by conduct most loyal to the truth and to
its defender, Athanasius. Called upon, by a message
from Constantius in A.D. 356, to condemn Athanasius,
Liberius insisted on demanding a fair trial for the
Bishop of Alexandria. He further demanded that
the accusers should disavow Arianism as a condition
of their being allowed to bring charges of misconduct
against the accused. Hereupon the emperor caused
Liberius to be forcibly brought from Milan, where he
was then staying, and undertook the task of converting
him by personal intercourse. A report of the conversation between the emperor and the bishop has
come down to us. Those are probably right who
hesitate to receive this document as thoroughly trustworthy. But there is no dispute about the main
result of the conference. Liberius rose in his demands. He called for a general subscription to the

[1] "De Unico Baptismo," one of its author's anti-Donatist
treatises (tom. ix., pp. 542, 543, in the Benedictine edition).

Nicene Creed, for the restoration of all banished
bishops, for a fair trial of Athanasius at Alexandria,
if trial there must needs be. Three days were then
allowed him, during which he was to decide whether
he would sign a document condemnatory of Athanasius, or depart into exile to such place as the emperor should name. Liberius did not hesitate, and
was accordingly sent to Berœa in Thrace. His spirited
conduct had, however, made an impression upon the
mind, not only of Constantius, but also upon that of
his Arian consort, the beautiful and accomplished
Aurelia Eusebia. They conjointly sent after Liberius
a present of a thousand pieces of gold. But he felt
that the acceptance of this gift would lay him under
some measure of obligation to the court. Consequently he refused it, and in a still more peremptory
manner declined aid from an imperial chamberlain,
the eunuch Eusebius.

It may also be considered as unquestioned, that
Liberius, at the time of his decease in A.D. 366, was
recognised as one who died in full communion with
the Church and among the defenders of the Catholic
faith.

But what is to be said as regards the intervening
time ? We have already implied, and it must now
again be repeated, that at the close of two years of
exile Liberius did in some degree, if the expression
may be allowed, lower his flag in token of surrender.
Not for one moment do we desire on such a theme
to employ a word that can seem to savour of un-
charitableness. Those alone who have felt the dreari-
ness of exile, or who have known what it is to suffer

imprisonment for conscience sake, have any right to speak upon the subject. That, among the hundred-and-forty-seven bishops banished by Constantius, only two of mark gave way, is a wonderful tribute to the general spirit of noble constancy and endurance. Liberius was sorely tried. He saw one of his own deacons, Felix by name, appointed bishop of Rome. Other bishops who had taken the side of the court, as Demophilus of Berœa, where Liberius was compelled to reside, and a man once thought brave and constant, Fortunatian, the bishop of Aquileia, urged him with subtle arguments. On one of the two points required of the exile, namely the condemnation of Athanasius, they plausibly represented that it did not involve any sacrifice of principle ; that, even if innocent of much that was laid to his charge, Athanasius was at best a wrong-headed man, who must be sacrificed, like another Jonah, for the sake of appeasing the storm which he had raised.

Let it be observed in passing, that the possibility of separating between a man and a cause must often be a reality, and that the case of Lucifer of Cagliari is an instance in point in connexion with the times of which we are writing. But, although we have not seen it thus stated, it appears to us that the career of the famous Bishop of Alexandria may, in this respect, be divided into two parts. During the first half of his episcopate, charges of misconduct were alleged against Athanasius with so much profusion and subtlety, that persons living at a distance might well suppose that he was really a turbulent and ill-judging man, nay, perhaps actually a criminal. But, as accusation after accusation proved groundless, the nobler spirits rapidly perceived wherein the real *gravamen* of the charges against Athanasius consisted. It lay in this, that misbelief and unbelief consisted in believing that the overthrow of the primate of Egypt was an absolute necessity. There were many elements of the struggle, which were greatly modified by the decease of the Arian Constantius and the accession of the Apostate Julian.   But this was not one of them. We have already quoted the emphatic words of Gibbon[1] respecting that sincere and peculiar hatred with which Julian honoured Athanasius. That this prince did not display equal enmity against Hilary lends countenance to the belief which the bishop of Poitiers entertained ; namely, that Saturninus, his chief opponent, had arraigned him, not on the ground of doctrine, but on that of political disloyalty, which Julian would probably know to be false, and would willingly disregard. But, among the foremost testimonies to the intimate connexion between the cause of Athanasius and the cause of truth, must ever be ranked the sentiments and conduct of the gifted Apostate.

It is hardly possible to believe that Liberius was not perfectly cognisant of what would be understood by acquiescence in the condemnation of Athanasius. But this was not the only condition exacted as the price of his return from captivity. As if to show that it was not a merely personal question that was at stake, he was called upon to subscribe a creed other than the Nicene Creed. The air was at that moment rife

"Decline and Fall," ch. xxiii.

with creeds. Their degrees of divergence from truth varied, but they were all non-Nicene ; they were all trying, if we may so speak, to dethrone that wonderful symbol of belief, and to occupy the vacant place. To sign this or that one might mean more or less ; might involve a profession of utter Arianism, or a subtle shade of difference which was capable of a good interpretation. But to sign any of these documents would be understood alike by friends and foes as in some degree an act of tergiversation.

What did Liberius do ? We answer in the words of St. Jerome's " Chronicle " : " Liberius, overcome by weariness of his banishment, *subscribed to heretical pravity*, and entered Rome as a conqueror." The same great doctor, in another work, his " Catalogue of Illustrious Men," expresses a natural feeling of indignation against the bishop of Aquileia—Fortunatian—who was a leading agent in the perversion of the Bishop of Rome. Jerome's account of this prelate, literally translated, runs as follows :—" Fortunatian, an African by birth, bishop of Aquileia in the reign of Constantine, wrote commentaries on the Gospels under duly arranged headings (*titulis ordinatis*) in a brief and homely style. On this ground he is regarded as an object of detestation (*habetur detestabilis*), that he was the first to solicit, and warp, *and force into an heretical subscription* Liberius, who had gone into exile for the sake of the faith."

We will give one more testimony. It is that of a virtual contemporary,[1] the historian Sozomen. Sozo-

[1] The historian Polybius, a great stickler for contemporary evidence, allows that a man may be a competent witness to

men declares that Constantius compelled Liberius to confess in public before a gathering of deputies from Eastern bishops and other presbyters that the Son is not of one substance with the Father.

Is there on this matter any counter-evidence? *Not one syllable.* It is possible, indeed, to allege the silence of two historians—Socrates and Theodôret. But this would prove too much. For Theodôret also omits the fall of Hosius of Cordova, about which, unhappily, there is neither doubt nor question. This puts Theodôret out of court, so to speak; and against the silence of Socrates we have not only the testimonies of St. Jerome, which have just been cited, but also that of an orthodox contemporary; Faustinus, and an Arian one, the historian Philostorgius.

The greatest remains. The writer of our own day who has more than any one else thoroughly sifted the evidence in this matter—Mr. P. le Page Renouf[1]—

events which happened twenty years before his birth. Sir G. C. Lewis, sympathising with Polybius, is yet inclined to give some extension to the time. He justly observes that many of us have heard much from grandfathers or persons of their generation, but that few of us have had any real acquaintance with our great-grandfathers. I should be inclined, from personal observation, to extend the limit to thirty-five years before birth. But the narrower term would, in this case, seemingly include Sozomen.

[1] In a note subjoined to his tractate, entitled, "The Condemnation of Pope Honorius." London : Longmans, 1868. The translator of Hefele's "History of the Councils" (Rev. H. N. Oxenham) has wisely and honourably reproduced this note (vol. ii., Edinburgh, Clark, 1876). We are immensely indebted to Mr. Renouf, and have verified the most important of his references.

most justly declares that "Athanasius speaks with the most noble tenderness of the fall both of Liberius and Hosius." And, indeed, Athanasius asserts a degree of peril as imminent over Liberius, which we do not find in any other history of the period. His words are :—"Liberius, after he had been in banishment two years, gave way, and *from fear of threatened death* was induced to subscribe" ("Arian History," sec. 41). Elsewhere this great confessor for the faith is found thoroughly to endorse the opinion which we had formed from other testimonies on the meaning at this juncture of a condemnation of Athanasius. For he quotes Constantius as having made the following avowal :—"Be persuaded, and subscribe against Athanasius ; for whoever subscribes against him thereby embraces with us the Arian cause."

Now it is certainly right for all of us who are not Roman Catholics to bear in mind that there is a possible danger of our consciously or unconsciously exaggerating the case against a pope ; especially since the Vatican Council has assigned to the Bishop of Rome the extraordinary powers now claimed for him. We have tried in this small volume to bear in mind this danger, and to remind our readers that the fall of Liberius was produced by threats, certainly of lifelong exile, possibly of death, and that there seems no reasonable doubt that he subsequently recovered himself.

But, if there be a danger on the one side, that danger is greatly intensified on the other. Up to A.D. 1500 the fall of Liberius had been unquestioned. But after the Reformation a great difference of tone

may be observed in certain quarters. One of the
authors known as the Bollandists (the compilers of
the still incomplete " Acta Sanctorum "), Stilting, attempted to disprove the charges made against Liberius ; and since the date of the Vatican Council the
attempt has been renewed by several anonymous
writers, and by one man of mark—Bishop Hefele.

This was, at any rate, a novelty. The whole of
the great Gallican school,—let it suffice to name Til-
lemont, Fleury, Montfauçon, Ceillier,—with one voice
proclaim the truth of the fall of Pope Liberius.
Möhler and Döllinger, the two greatest names among
German Roman Catholics, are on the same side.
M. Renouf (who was a Roman Catholic before the
question of papal infallibility was brought up in connexion with the Vatican Council) not only cites the
famous Italian controversialist, Cardinal Bellarmine,
as equally explicit with the French and German in-
quirers, but declares that the various mediæval mar-
tyrologies contained distinct reference to the fall of
Liberius ; nay, more, that it was not until the sixteenth century that they were struck out of the Roman
Breviary. Its words are, indeed, most emphatic on
the assent rendered by the Bishop of Rome to Arian
heresy.

And now to come back to the question of the
evidence rendered by the historic fragments of Hilary.
Even if, with Dom Ceillier and with the Benedictine
editor of Hilary, Dom Coutant, we forbear to press
some of the documents as being questionable, there
remains enough to show how strongly Hilary felt upon
the subject. Yet more ; the interjections from his

pen tend to prove either that he must have regarded the concessions to the bishop of Rome made by the Council of Sardica as peculiar to Julius, or else that he recorded them as an historic judgment to which larger experience of life forbade his practical assent.

If any assert that Liberius did not fall, they may as well give up all belief in history. To say that his utterances during the period of his lapse, having been brought about by threats, cannot be regarded as the deliberate verdicts of a bishop of Rome, is intelligible. But it seems impossible to regard them as the mere private enunciations. It was in order to free himself from exile, possibly to save his life, certainly to regain his see, that Liberius yielded. The defence that he was only writing as a private doctor was unheard of before the present century, and a Roman Catholic dignitary, Cardinal de la Luzerne,[1] has distinctly asserted the contrary. His words seem important, and will make a fitting termination to the present chapter :—" He gave what was demanded of him on the conditions on which it was demanded. When they demanded his signature at the hand of a pope, as pope, it is the pope, as pope, who gave it." Of the subscription given by Liberius to another creed than the Nicene, the Cardinal says, " this was only the beginning of his fall ; it is not by a single act, but by a succession, that he manifestly declared himself heretical." We take no pleasure in the fall of any one, least of all of a chief shepherd of Christ's flock.

[1] We translate from the pamphlet of Mr. Renouf. The correctness of his quotations makes him in such a matter thoroughly trustworthy.

M

But facts are facts, and history is history. We see
no escape from the conclusions herein laid down ;
although, as we have already remarked, it is satisfactory to reflect that Liberius returned to his old
allegiance, again contended for the Catholic faith,
and died in full communion with its children and
champions.

CHAPTER XV.

MINOR ELUCIDATIONS.

IT is proposed in this chapter to touch briefly upon two or three incidental topics on which it is impossible, within the limits of this work, to dwell with fulness. We refer more especially (1) to the ideas of Hilary as a commentator deducible from the compilation made by the famous schoolman, Aquinas; (2) to some features in one of his latest struggles, that against the Arian bishop of Milan, Auxentius; and (3) to his position in the field of hymnology.

1. St. Thomas Aquinas, amongst his many remarkable contributions to theology, gave us a commentary upon the four Gospels woven with extraordinary skill out of the works of the ancient Fathers. It possesses some of the defects natural to the period of its production. Quotations are occasionally given which later editors, particularly the Benedictines, have since discovered to be spurious. It is also possible that to some modern readers the allegorical interpretations may seem to occupy a disproportionate place among the links of this " Golden Chain." In the case of the extracts made from Hilary this element is, we incline to think, unduly prominent. Nevertheless, as opinions on such a point may fairly differ, it seems right to make a slight addition to the cursory notice given in a

former chapter, and to cite a few specimens of Hilary as an allegorist, if such a term may be permitted. It must be premised that in this department of interpretation Hilary is certainly, on the whole, inferior to some other Fathers in felicity, more especially to Origen. We, of course, select one or two of our author's most successful efforts.

The following is Hilary's comment on our Lord's discourse concerning the work and office of the holy Baptist, recorded in the eleventh chapter of St. Matthew :—

" In these things which were done concerning John there is a deep store of mystic meaning. The very condition and circumstances of a prophet are themselves a prophecy. John signifies the Law : for the Law proclaimed Christ, preaching remission of sins, and giving promise of the kingdom of heaven. Also when the Law was on the point of expiring (having been through the sins of the people, which hindered them from understanding what it spake of Christ, as it were, shut up in bonds and in prison), it sends men to the contemplation of the Gospel that unbelief might see the truth of its words established by deeds."

Here is a similar application of the parable concerning the grain of mustard-seed (St. Matt. xiii., 31–32) :—

" This grain, then, when sown in the field,—that is, when seized by the people and delivered to death, and, as it were, buried in the ground by a sowing of the body,—grew up beyond the size of all herbs, and exceeded all the glory of the Prophets. For the preaching of the Prophets was allowed, as if it were herbs, to a sick man; but now the birds of the air lodge in the branches of the tree; by which we understand the Apostles, who put forth of Christ's might, and overshadowing the world with their boughs, are a tree to which the Gentiles flee in hope of life, and having been long tossed by the winds (that is, by the spirits of the devil), may have rest in its branches."

Hilary occasionally dwells, in common with many of the Fathers, upon the supposed suggestiveness of the numbers mentioned in connexion with some incident. Thus, for example, as regards the miraculous feeding first of the five thousand and then of the four thousand, he observes :—

"As that first multitude which He fed answers to the people among the Jews that believed, so this is compared to the people of the Gentiles, the number of four quarternions denoting an innumerable number of people out of the four quarters of the earth."

It cannot, we think, be affirmed that any marked success has attended investigations of this sort respecting the mystic meaning of numbers. The subject possesses a great charm, however, for certain minds. Such a belief formed a leading element in one of the most high-toned systems of ancient philosophy,—that of the Pythagoreans. Plato has also shown a disposition to encourage it, though his references to the subject are far from being clear and intelligible. In modern physical science the discoveries of Dalton in chemistry are connected with numbers to a degree that is almost marvellous.[1] If there be mysteries

[1] The following account is abridged from the "Religio Chemici" of a very delightful writer, the late Professor George

entwined with numbers in nature, it is also possible that the same law may hold good with reference to revelation. But when it has been remarked that certain numbers,—as, for example, *seven* and *forty*, recur very frequently in the pages of Holy Writ; that some mystery may underlie such a fact; and that such belief is commonly manifested in patriotic theology, and has had a certain measure of influence upon Christian art, we have probably said all that can be safely advanced at present. No consistent theory upon this matter has yet been proved.

And here we leave this part of Hilary's exposition, merely adding that though Aquinas may have given

Wilson, in his essay on the life and discoveries of Dalton (Macmillan, 1862, pp. 309–322). The laws of proportional combination are universally received as true by chemists. They are four in number. 1. The same elements which form a chemical compound are always united in it in the same proportion by weight. 2. When one body combines with another in several proportions, the higher ones are multiples of the first or lowest. 3. If two bodies combine in certain proportions with a third, they combine in the very same proportions with each other. 4. The combining proportion of a compound body is the sum of the combining proportions of its components. Dr. Wilson was a thorough scientist, though a poetical one. A more purely poetical view of the matter is given in Longfellow's tale "Kavanagh " (chap. iv.), "'I do not see how you can make mathematics poetical. There is no poetry in them." "Ah ! that is a very great mistake. There is something divine in the science of numbers. Like God, it holds the sea in the hollow of its hand. It measures the earth ; it weighs the stars ; it illumines the universe ; it is law, it is order, it is beauty." Perhaps these extracts, and the strange passage in Plato's " Republic " (liber viii., cap. 3), may help to account for the fascination exercised by numbers on certain theologians.

it undue prominence, he has not wholly excluded specimens of our author's more usual comments. We give one merely by way of example. Hilary is expounding the confession of St. Peter (St. Matt. xvi. 16) :—

"This is the true and unalterable faith, that from God came forth God the Son, who has eternity out of the eternity of the Father. That this God took unto Him a body, and was made man, is a perfect confession. Thus he embraced all, in that He here expresses both His nature and His name, in which is the sum of virtues. This confession of Peter met a worthy reward, for that he had seen the Son of God in the man."

2. There is an obvious reason for not dwelling much on the details of Hilary's contest with Auxentius. We fear that our readers may be rather wearied with continuous accounts of the struggles against Arianism; although it is well that they should bear in mind on this theme the admonition of a writer not generally disposed to over-value the work of the champions of orthodoxy. "That wonderful metaphysic subtlety," wrote Charles Kingsley, "which, in phrases and definitions too often unmeaning to our grosser intellect, saw the symbols of the most important spiritual realities, and felt that on the distinction between *homoousios* and *homoiousios* might hang the solution of the whole problem of humanity, was set to battle in Alexandria, the ancient stronghold of Greek philosophy, with the effete remains of the very scientific thought to which it owed its extraordinary culture. Monastic isolation from family and national duties

especially fitted the fathers of that period for the
task, by giving them leisure, if nothing else, to face
questions with a life-long earnestness impossible to
the mere social and practical northern mind. *Our
duty is, instead of sneering at them as pedantic dreamers,
to thank Heaven that men were found, just at the time
when they were wanted, to do for us what we could
never have done for ourselves; to leave us as a precious
heirloom, bought most truly with the life-blood of their
race, a metaphysic at once Christian and scientific, every
attempt to improve on which has hitherto been found a
failure;* and to battle victoriously with that strange
brood of theoretic monsters begotten by effete Greek
philosophy upon Egyptian symbolism, Chaldee astro-
logy, Parsee dualism, Brahminic spiritualism." It
is true that Kingsley is chiefly thinking of the East;
but Hilary was, as we have seen, the representative
champion of the same contest in the West.[1]

It is right to observe, before we proceed, that
Auxentius is one of the few persons against whom
the bishop of Milan employs severity of language.
Now, to record all Hilary's expressions would almost
inevitably convey a very false impression to the mind
of any ordinary reader. For the amount of objurgation contained in Hilary's writings, taken as a whole,
is not very large, and to set down everything of the
kind in this small work would give a most unjust
impression of the proportionate space which it occu-
pies in his writings. Three persons only seem to
be special objects of his indignation,—Saturninus,

---

[1] Preface to Hypatia (p. xv.). We are quoting from the
tenth edition (London: Macmillan & Co., 1878).

Constantius, and Auxentius. But, in all these cases, it was not heresy or the patronage of heresy which alone moved the wrath of Hilary; it was the combination, in his judgment, of utter dishonesty with misbelief.

Towards the close of A.D. 364, the altercation between the two prelates attracted the observation of Valentinian, who had become emperor soon after the commencement of that year. Both from such evidence as remains to us, and from the generally charitable estimate of opponents formed by Hilary, there seems good ground for believing that his judgment of Auxentius was just. But, inasmuch as, though seeming Arian in his heart, Auxentius made a profession of orthodoxy, we can hardly wonder that Valentinian acted as most rulers and statesmen would have been inclined to act under similar circumstances, and declined to examine the accusations made by Hilary. Indeed, the emperor openly entered into communion with Auxentius, and ordered Hilary to leave Milan. Hilary obeyed the imperial mandate without delay, but once more betook himself to his pen. Into the arguments whereby he seeks to prove the covert Arianism of his fellow bishop, we do not propose to enter; but two points outside the personal controversy deserve attention.

One of these points has already come before us in the discussion contained in an earlier chapter, namely, chapter ix., concerning Hilary and the emperor. Of the two courses which had been alternately followed by Constantius, persecution and the allurement of flattery, Valentinian, in Hilary's judgment, seemed inclined to adopt the gentle one. But this was a special object of dread to Hilary; indeed, so much so as to render him perhaps rather one-sided in his sentiments and language concerning it. Like many other excellent men, he had a keen sense of the actual danger then impending, and was consequently rather inclined to underrate the terrible trials which had existed for ordinary Christians during the previous ages of persecution.

The second point is one of those which lend some countenance to the much-mooted proposition, "History repeats itself." Hilary saw reason to fear that the defenders of the Catholic faith in Milan might be tempted to enter into some compromise with its opponents, for the sake of keeping possession of some cherished and valued places of worship. On this topic Hilary is most emphatic. "Specious indeed is the name of peace and fair the very thought of unity; but who can doubt that that unity of the church and of the gospels alone is peace which preserves the unity of Christ,—that peace of which He spoke to the Apostles after His glorious Passion, which on the eve of departure He commended to us for a pledge of His eternal mandate,—that peace, brethren most beloved, which we have endeavoured to seek when it has been lost, to smooth when it has been disturbed, to hold fast when it has been found ? But to become partakers or creators of this kind of peace has been denied to us by the sins of our age, has been disallowed by the forerunners and ministers of an impending antichrist, men who exult in a peace of their own, that is to say in a unity of impiety, who conduct themselves not as bishops of Christ, but as priests of antichrist."

Hilary gives a short explanation of the way in which there may be many antichrists, as St. John has taught us in his first Epistle (ii. 18). He proceeds to lament the tendency to court the patronage of emperors and officers of state, which is in fashion.

" And first allow me to pity the toil of our age, and to bewail the foolish opinions of the present day, in which men believe that human powers can patronise God, and endeavour to defend the church of Christ by a worldly ambition. Fain would I ask you, O ye bishops, who believe that such a course is possible, what sort of aids did the Apostles employ in furtherance of their preaching of the gospel? by what powers were they helped when they preached Christ, and turned well-nigh all nations from idols to God? Did they seek to win any honour from the palace when they were singing a hymn in prison in chains after their scourging? Was it by the edict of a king that Paul laboured to gather together a church for Christ, at the time when he was a spectacle in the theatre for men to gaze upon? Was he, do you suppose, defended by the patronage of a Nero, a Vespasian, or a Decius, men who by their hatred against us made the confession of the divine messages to bud forth? The apostles, who supported themselves by the labours of their own hands, who met together in upper chambers and in secret places, who traversed towns and fortresses and well-nigh all nations by land and sea in the teeth of decrees of the senate and mandates of kings—did they, forsooth, not hold

the keys of the kingdom of heaven ? Rather, did not
the power of God then manifestly exhibit itself
against human hatred, when Christ was all the more
preached in proportion as that preaching was for-
bidden ? " [1]

Hilary proceeds to analyse the many evasions, of
which Auxentius was guilty both as regards doctrine
and fact ; as, for example, his denial that he knew
Arius, when in truth he had commenced his career
as a presbyter in Alexandria at an Arian Church,
presided over by one Gregory. The desire of the
Emperor Valentinian not to stir up awkward inquiries,
and to assume the sincerity of all who professed to be
orthodox, seemed but too likely in time to infect the
flocks. It might happen that if they opposed the
Emperor's views (not, as we have remarked, unnatural
views for a statesman to adopt) they might incur the
danger to which we have referred, and lose possession
of the churches. Hilary, as we have remarked, is
most anxious to forewarn them on the peril of such
an anxiety. He shrinks from committing to paper all
the disgraceful blasphemies of the Arians.

"But one warning I give you : be on your guard
against antichrist. A dangerous affection for walls
has seized upon you ; in a mistaken way you venerate
the Church of God as if it must be seated under roofs
and in buildings, and you connect with such things
the idea of peace. But is there a doubt but that
antichrist will take his seat in these? To my thinking,
the mountains and the woods and lakes, the very

[1] The reference in Hilary's mind is evidently to 2 Thessalo-
nians ii. 3, 4.

prisons and chasms, are safer; for in such places men of old, either abiding by choice or detained by force, used to prophecy by the Spirit of God. Keep away then from Auxentius, the Angel of Satan, the enemy of Christ, the abandoned devastator, the denier of the faith; who has made to the Emperor a profession framed in order to mislead; who has deceived in such wise as to blaspheme. Let him now collect against me what synods he chooses; and publicly proscribe me as a heretic, as he has often done; let him stir up against me at his liking the wrath of the powerful. To me assuredly he will always be a Satan, because he is an Arian. Nor shall peace ever be desired save the peace of those who, according to the creed of our fathers at Nicæa, anathematize Arians and preach Christ as true God."

3. For convenience sake and from a desire that this chapter may not close with accents of fiery controversy, we have disregarded chronological exactness. For the struggle with Auxentius took place after Hilary's return from banishment, whereas the hymn to which we now invite attention was composed during its author's exile, and was enclosed in a letter to his daughter Abra. It cannot indeed be pretended that the one specimen of this kind of composition, of which the genuineness seems the best established, is such as to place the Bishop of Poitiers on a level with St. Ambrose, far less with some of the mediæval writers of hymns. Still it is singular that the earliest Latin hymn, to which we are able to assign a name as that of its author, should be the work of that Father of the Church who gave us the earliest treatise

upon the doctrine of the Holy Trinity and the first
commentary upon a Gospel. As will be seen from
the following attempt to render it, it is addressed
to the Second Person of the Holy Trinity, and is
rightly called a *Morning Hymn :—*

Radiant Giver of the light,
   By whose calm and piercing ray,
When have flown the hours of night,
   Comes the re-awakening day ;

True enlightener of the earth,
   Not like feeble morning-star,
Herald of the sun-light's birth,
   Dimly brooding from afar,

But brighter than the noon-tide blaze,
   Fount and source of all our day,
Potent in men's heart to raise
   Sparks that ne'er shall fade away.

Framer of the realms of space,
   Glory of Thy Father's light,
Teach, by treasures of Thy grace,
   Hearts to scan themselves aright.

Still the Spirit's aid impart,
   Make us shrines of the Most High,
Lest the arch-rebel traitor's art
   Lure us by its witchery.

Earthly needs of life entail
   Daily cares without, within ;
Make Thy precepts still prevail,
   Guide us through them free from sin.

Lawless passion's force repress,
   Purity of heart bestow ;
E'en our mortal bodies bless
   Th' Holy Spirit's shrines to grow.

Thus the prayerful soul aspires,
Such its votive-gifts to Thee,
Trusting that thy morn-lit fires
Serve for nightly custody.[1]

---

[1] Some copies contain a doxology, but this is probably a later addition.

CHAPTER XVI.

LAST YEARS OF HILARY—CONCLUSION.

THE decision of Constantius, which had sent Hilary back to Gaul, though still keeping the sentence of banishment hanging over him, allowed him some freedom in his mode of return. It was dilatory, for he stayed at various places on the road, and his happiness at the prospect of regaining home was much alloyed by the scenes which he witnessed. The emperor had banished from their sees all the bishops who refused to accept the ambiguous form of words set forth by the Council of Rimini, and many flocks were mourning the absence of their chief pastors. The year 361 was spent in this way; but in the following year Hilary regained his home, and rejoined his wife and daughter. He was warmly welcomed by the inhabitants of his native town and by the diocese at large, and his friend and disciple, Martin of Tours, was among those who hastened to visit him.

Abra had received addresses during his absence; and he, on hearing it, had sent her a letter of a rather mystic though exceedingly affectionate character. Its tendency was to set forth the superiority of celibacy. But he wished the decision to be really her own, though if she found any difficulty in understanding his letter, or two hymns which he enclosed, she was to consult her mother. He found her unwedded on his return, and she may probably have remained so.

The more ardent among Hilary's friends and supporters desired, as has been observed already, to refuse communion to all who had been betrayed into the acceptance of the decrees of Rimini. .But such a course did not commend itself to their leader. Hilary preferred the plan of gathering together, in different parts of Gaul, assemblies of bishops, and entering into mutual explanations. The line proposed by him proved most successful, and the counter-efforts of his old opponent, Saturninus, were utterly fruitless. The Bishop of Arles found himself thoroughly deserted, and was in a short time practically excluded from communion with the Gallican episcopate.

The attempt to carry out still further this line of conduct by a journey into Northern Italy and Illyria was not, as we have implied, equally successful. Though Eusebius of Vercelli lent Hilary powerful aid, the efforts of these two friends seem to have been threatened by the conduct of the well-intentioned, but uncompromising, Lucifer of Cagliari. Nevertheless, Hilary remained in Italy from the latter part of A.D. 362 until the late autumn of 364, when, as has already been mentioned, he was ordered home by the Emperor Valentinian. Ten years later, had he lived so long, Hilary would have had the satisfaction of seeing Ambrose become bishop of Milan.

The last three or four years of his life were spent at Poitiers, and seemed to have been comparatively quiet

N

and untroubled.   He died in peace on January 13th,[1]
A.D. 368.

There was so much of paganism remaining in Gaul
at the date of Hilary's conversion, that he might
have, humanly speaking, enjoyed a brilliant career as
a member of the gifted, and, for those times, polished
society of the aristocracy of his native land.   In that
case, he would not have known exile; and, though
he might have disliked many of the anti-pagan measures of Constantius, he probably would not have
protested against them any more than did the heathen
orators of the day, such as Themistius or Libanius,
who continued to lavish flatteries upon the emperor,
though in their hearts believing him to be an enemy
of the gods.   But there was that in Hilary which,
by the grace of God, rendered such a career impossible; and his country, and Christendom at large,
more especially in the West, were to be the gainers.
Even in Britain a few churches have been dedicated
to his memory.   The great popularity of the name
Hilaire in France is a tribute to the impression which
he made upon the public mind.   This impression may
have been deepened by the good gifts of his namesake, St. Hilary of Arles, in the succeeding century.

But we can hardly look back upon Hilary's
troubled and chequered career, noble as it was, without feeling that it offers one of the numerous illustrations of the fact, that in whatever age of the
Church our lot might have been cast we should

[1] The date of January 14th, assigned to his festival in the
Roman service books, is simply an alteration made for convenience sake, the 13th being the Octave of the Epiphany.

have found difficulties at least as great as those of our own time. In the eighteenth century its spiritual deadness might have paralysed us. In the sixteenth we should have had to undergo the fierce trial of deciding, not merely between Mediævalism and the Reformation, but between, it may be, the different schools and theories of reform. In the fifteenth, we might have shared its torpor, or have become intoxicated with the pagan spirit of the movement known as the *Renaissance*. In the early part of the thirteenth century, a wave of unbelief, exceedingly mysterious in its origin, and as subtle as anything to which we are now exposed, might have swept us away in its vortex. And, during the first three centuries, there might have been presented to us the choice between apostasy and a death of torture, demanding heroic virtue to support it.

And how, as regards that age, the middle of the fourth century, in which was placed, by God's providence, the life of Hilary of Poitiers? He has himself described it.

"It is a thing equally deplorable and dangerous that there are as many creeds as opinions among men, as many doctrines as inclinations, and as many sources of blasphemy as there are faults among us, because we make creeds arbitrarily and explain them arbitrarily. The Homöusion is rejected, and received, and explained away by successive synods. The partial or total resemblance of the Father and of the Son is a subject of dispute for these unhappy times. Every year, nay, every moon, we make new creeds to describe invisible mysteries. We repent of what we have done, we defend those who repent, we anathematise those whom we defended. We condemn either the doctrine of others in ourselves, or our own in that of others; and, reciprocally tearing one another to pieces, we have been the cause of each other's ruin."

That, unlike these varying creeds, the Nicene Creed has endured, is, as we have already remarked, a wonderful tribute to the divine blessing on the work of the famous council which drew it up.

That Hilary was permitted to take an honourable, and, on the whole, a wonderfully successful part in bringing Christendom out of this state of chaos, and that his character and conduct were not unworthy of his lofty aims and devout writings, form his title to our reverence and regard,—

> We live by admiration, hope, and love,
> And even as these are well and wisely fix'd
> In dignity of being we ascend.[1]

One alone, indeed, of our race can satisfy all the demands of the human heart, and intellect, and conscience. But His servants stand around Him, and lead onward to Him. To throw our lot with them is to hope for acceptance at His hands :—

> Thou art the King of Glory, O Christ,
> Thou art the everlasting Son of the Father.
> We therefore pray Thee help Thy servants, whom Thou
> hast redeemed with Thy precious blood.
> Make them to be numbered with Thy saints in glory
> everlasting.

---

[1] Wordsworth.

ST. MARTIN OF TOURS.

ST. MARTIN OF TOURS.

CHAPTER I.

INTRODUCTORY.

MARTIN, commonly known as St. Martin of Tours, appears to have been a contemporary of St. Hilary of Poitiers. We say appears to have been, because the chronology of Martin's life is sadly confused. In all probability he was born before Hilary, and lived some twenty-eight years after Hilary's death, his long life of eighty years extending from A.D. 316–396. As, however, Hilary was not only the more learned, but may have formed his theological convictions sooner, the tradition which speaks of Martin as a pupil of Hilary need not be incorrect or incredible. Twice, at least, Martin paid a visit to Hilary. Both became bishops of sees in Gaul, at no very great distance from each other, Tours and Poitiers being only separated by a space of some sixty miles. Both were converts from heathenism to Christianity; both became champions on behalf of the faith as against unbelief and misbelief; both made a great impress upon their age, and occupy a prominent place in the Church's annals.

But although they were sympathetic friends, and aimed at the like objects, the points of contrast are almost more numerous and more marked than those of resemblance.

The social position of Hilary by birth was a rather high one; that of Martin was what was considered respectable, but not more. Hilary struggled chiefly against *mis*-belief, that is to say, against heresy among Christians; Martin's labours were more especially directed against *un*-belief, against the heathenism of Gaul. Hilary was husband and father; Martin a celibate and monk. Hilary was the author of large and able treatises on theology and commentaries on holy Scripture; Martin hardly wrote anything, and we do not possess a page that can safely be ascribed to his pen. But although Hilary's writings have furnished material for the study of famous theologians of after-age, such as a Jerome, an Erasmus, a Dorner, the work of Martin, who has left no written word, made a still livelier impression upon the heart and imagination, not only of Gaul, but of Western Christendom at large.

Another point of difference emerges at the outset of any attempt to sketch the career of these two allies. The events of the life of Hilary can be almost entirely gathered from his own writings. The genuineness of the main facts is unquestioned. Moreover, although in one passage of his works Hilary recognises the occurrence of some miracles at the tombs of martyrs, he does not anywhere so much as allude, to the best of our belief, to any supernatural marvel in connexion with his own history. In regard to Martin, the case is precisely the reverse. The one main authority for his biography is his friend and pupil, Sulpicius Severus. He was a writer of some elegance, and one who, if he possessed little idea of historic proportion, was fairly trustworthy as a witness to the ordinary events of life. But, in regard to the supernatural, he belongs to a large class of writers, whom it is impossible to regard as safe narrators of literal fact. An explanation of the point of view adopted on this subject in the following pages seems to require for its treatment a separate chapter.

CHAPTER II.

MIRACLES IN THE POST-APOSTOLIC AGES.

IN sketches of history offered to Christian readers by Christian writers, it must be lawful to assume, without argument, certain propositions, which are held by the overwhelming majority of those who profess and call themselves Christians.

Accordingly, it will here be assumed, that to speak of a "non-miraculous Christianity" is to speak of something utterly at variance with the Christianity known and recognised as such for nearly nineteen hundred years. "The Gospel," it has been truly said, "is but one tissue of supernatural events. The Gospel is the supernatural itself. The Gospel is the birth of a Virgin's Son. The Gospel is the resurrection of One dead. It begins and ends in miracle."[1] .

We assume, also, that our Lord promised to his immediate followers the continuance of miraculous powers. The book of the Acts of the Apostles recounts many manifestations of the fulfilment of this promise. In other parts of the New Testament, as, for example, the Epistles to the Romans and to the

[1] Essay, "How to ascertain the Gospel facts," in an Appendix to the first volume of "The Church and the Empire in the Fourth Century," by the Duc de Broglie (Paris, 1857).

Hebrews, distinct appeal is made to this feature of apostolic labours.[1]

When, however, we descend lower down the stream of history, say from A.D. 300, the commencement of the fourth century, to the period of the Reformation, we find that there has been engendered in Christendom an atmosphere of intense credulity in these matters. In what are called the Middle Ages,—say roughly A.D. 400–1300,—the biography of a holy man, even that of an Athanasius or a Hilary, would seem to lack an essential characteristic if it did not contain the record of marvels wrought by the saint.

Now, credulity is not faith. It may even become the enemy of faith. When Henry Martyn began speaking to the Persians of the Great Teacher, in whose name he came to them, he told them how the Prophet of prophets had given evidence of His divine mission by many marvels; amongst others by recalling three persons from the dead. His auditors replied that this was nothing at all; they had possessed a sage who wrought this miracle on a large scale, having raised from the dead some hundreds. A Roman Catholic writer of our age, a French barrister, who has written with great ability and power on the side of belief, has been struck with the difficulty thus created. In his chapter on miracles

---

[1] "Things which Christ wrought through me, for the obedience of the Gentiles, by word and deed, *in the power of signs and wonders*, in the power of the Holy Ghost."—Romans xv. 18, 19 (Revised Version). "God also bearing witness with them, *both by signs and wonders*, and by manifold powers, and by gifts of the Holy Ghost."—Hebrews ii. 4 (Revised Version).

this author, M. Nicolas, feels that in defending the Gospel miracles he is compelled to face the fact of "the false miracles, which, in the Middle Ages were accepted so easily, and met with so little criticism."[1]

We may well suppose that, in a vast number of cases, the narrators of marvels which will not bear critical examination had no intention to deceive.

In the first place, during these ages physical science was all but unknown. Such appearances as drops of moisture oozing out of marble pillars might be in good faith interpreted as marks of sorrow for some martyr's death by spectators who had not observed them at other times. A miracle of this nature is reported by an early Church historian.

Often, no doubt, the border line between the natural and the supernatural is hard to draw. Few facts in history are better attested than the failure of the apostate Julian to rebuild the Temple at Jerusalem,—a project whereby he hoped to prove the falsity of at least one prophecy of the Divine Founder of Christianity. It was stopped by an outburst of fire, which thoroughly alarmed the workmen. Even the heathen historian, Ammianus Marcellinus, admits thus much. With the majority of Christian historians the present writer is inclined to regard this event as decidedly miraculous. Nevertheless, it is possible, as Döllinger seems inclined to believe, that there may have been an explosion of what is now called fire-damp. Still, even in that case Divine Fore-

---

[1] See an article on "Supernatural Religion and the Rationale of Miracles" in No. III. of the "Church Quarterly Review" (April, 1876).

knowledge may have so arranged the resources of nature, as that an outburst of stored-up forces at that particular juncture should bring about the desired result. Julian, so to speak, threw down a gauntlet to Christ. The challenge was accepted; the Temple remained a ruin.

Many remarkable answers to prayer must lie very near the border line between the natural and the miraculous.

There is another large class of narratives wherein marvels seem to have been related as allegorical representations of the struggles of grace against sin. This is admitted by learned and candid writers of the Roman Catholic communion; as, for instance, Möhler and the Duc de Broglie. The latter compares the narratives told concerning the Fathers of the desert to the "Pilgrim's Progress" of John Bunyan.

It is also obvious that in many cases the impression made upon the human mind would, in a practical point of view, be the same, whether a given appearance were the result of a sensitive imagination or an outward reality. Dr. Doddridge has told us how Colonel Gardiner was converted by a seeming vision, and the account has been more widely read in consequence of its introduction by Sir Walter Scott into the notes to "Waverley." The effect upon Gardiner's life was the same, whether the appearance was something outward (or, in scholastic language, *objective*), or a fancy of Gardiner's own creation. A Protestant historian of this century, M. Guizot, has declared that in the earlier Middle Age,—he

makes special reference to the seventh century :—
" The spectacle of the events that were happening
day by day revolted or repressed all the moral
instincts of man ; everything seemed given up to
chance or force ; nowhere could men find in the
external world that empire of rule, that idea of duty,
that respect for right, which make the security of life
and the repose of the soul. *They found them in
legends."* M. Guizot gives a specimen, which involves
a protest against the sale of slaves, and then adds,
" Exaggeration in the details is of small importance ;
*even the material truth of the history would be of small
importance ;* it was written at the commencement of
the seventh century ; it was told to men of the
seventh century. You see what a charm for them
this simple narrative must have possessed. It was a
real moral consolation ; a protestation against hateful
and dominant facts ; a feeble, but precious, re-echo
of the rights of liberty." Great allowance must, no
doubt, be made for states of mind when an English
historian[1] has said "the distinction between objective
and subjective truth has no existence," though many
of us may agree with Canon Liddon in regarding this
state of mind, albeit compatible with earnest piety,
as involving special dangers of its own.

Shall it be said that, after taking into account the
whole of these sources of error, we may safely conclude that *all* the narratives of miracles related in the
lifetime of the saints are fabulous ? Speaking merely
for himself, the present writer is unable to accept this

---

[1] Mr. Froude.

position. He does not see any proof in the nature of things, or in the page of Holy Scripture, that miracles must have ceased with the death of the last apostle ; and it is evident that, if some real miracles were vouchsafed to a Martin or a Columba, the inclination to accept too readily the report of other marvels less well authenticated would receive a powerful and wide-spread impulse.

Some forty years ago an audience in Oxford was listening to a professor of modern history, who discussed this subject. After pointing out the difference between the Gospel miracles and those recorded by ecclesiastical historians, the lecturer proceeded as follows :—" Some appear to be unable to conceive of belief, or unbelief, except as having some ulterior object : 'we believe this, because we love it ; we disbelieve it, because we wish it to be disproved.' There is, however, in minds more healthfully constituted a belief, and a disbelief, grounded solely upon the evidence of the case, arising neither out of partiality nor out of prejudice against the supposed conclusions, which may result from its truth or falsehood. And in such a spirit the historical student will consider the case of Bede's and other historians' miracles. He will, I think, as a general rule, disbelieve them ; for the immense multitude which he finds recorded, and which, I suppose, no credulity could believe in, shows sufficiently that on this point there was a total want of judgment and a blindness of belief generally existing which make the testimony wholly insufficient ; and, while the external evidence in favour of these alleged miracles is so unsatisfactory, there are, for the most part, strong internal improbabilities against them.   But with regard to some miracles, he will see that there is no strong *à priori* improbability in their occurrence, but rather the contrary ; as, for instance, when the first missionaries of the Gospel in a barbarous country are said to have been assisted by a manifestation of the spirit of power ; and, if the evidence appears to warrant his belief, he will readily and gladly yield it.   And in doing so he will have the countenance of a great man [Edmund Burke] who, in his fragment of English history, has not hesitated to express the same sentiments.   Nor will he be unwilling, but most thankful, to find sufficient grounds for believing that not only at the beginning of the Gospel, but in ages long afterwards, believing prayer has received extraordinary answers ; that it has been heard even in more than it might have dared to ask for.   Yet, again, if the gift of faith—the gift as distinguished from the grace—of the faith which removes mountains, has been given to any in later times in remarkable measure, the mighty works which such faith may have wrought cannot be incredible in themselves to those who remember our Lord's promise, and if it appears from satisfactory evidence that they were wrought actually, we shall believe them—and believe with joy.   Only as it is in most cases impossible to admit the trustworthiness of the evidence, our minds must remain at the most in a state of suspense ; and I do not know why it is necessary to come to any positive decision."

The above words made a great impression upon the mind of at least one person who listened to them ;

not the less so, perhaps, because he hardly expected to hear them from the lips of the speaker, Dr. Arnold of Rugby.

That person is now addressing the reader, and it is in such a spirit that the miracles attributed to St. Martin will be regarded in the following pages.

CHAPTER III.

YOUTH OF MARTIN.

In a settled state of society the deepest impression upon the inhabitants of a country is usually made by a native. But in the conversion of a people from heathenism to Christianity the largest part of the work has been frequently accomplished by the efforts of some stranger. The name of Martin must ever stand prominent among those who helped to make Gaul a part of Christendom. But Martin was not a Gaul by birth. He was born at a place called Sabaria, in the country now known as Lower Hungary. His parents were both heathen. Their names have not come down to us. But his father was a soldier, and apparently a successful one, inasmuch as he rose to the honourable rank of a military tribune. The legion to which he belonged was stationed for a considerable time at Pavia, in North Italy. In that city Martin received his education. It was probably not of a very deep or extended character, and it appears to have been purely pagan.

But there are times when certain ideas are, so to speak, in the air, and find an entrance, by divine favour, into what might seem at first sight unlikely places. We honour the soldier, it has been well said, "not because he slays, but because he is willing to be slain ;"[1] and certainly the profession of arms, which in many respects is so full of temptation, does often, especially in active service, involve stern lessons of obedience, patience, and the discipline of suffering.[2] Few callings receive more honourable notice in the pages of the New Testament. Soldiers are among those who seek instruction from the lips of the Great Preacher of repentance in the wilderness of Judæa. It is a Roman centurion who displays a faith which our Lord had not met with even in Israel; it is another centurion who recognises the righteousness of the Crucified One by the marvels which accompany His death; and a third centurion, Cornelius, has the glory of being the first convert to Christianity from heathenism.

Milan, which is not far from Pavia, was a great centre of Christian life, and there were, no doubt, many opportunities of coming into contact with orthodox Christians and their ways and thoughts throughout the north of Italy; although, as we see from the life of St. Hilary and that of St. Ambrose, Arianism displayed considerable energy in those parts in the fourth century. If we adopt A.D. 316 as the probable date of Martin's birth, it must have been in A.D. 326 that Martin, then in his tenth year, fled from his parents, and got enrolled among the number of *catechumens*, or of converts desirous of

[1] Ruskin.
[2] "There is more godliness in camp than in barracks."— Archibald Forbes, War Correspondent of the *Daily News* and other journals. A French soldier, M. Paul de Molènes, entirely corroborates Mr. A. Forbes's statement.

being instructed and prepared for holy baptism. Left to himself, Martin would, even then, most probably have soon joined some monastic community. But his parents interposed their authority, and some five years later the father was enabled from his position in the army to bring down upon his son the weight of an imperial edict. This was a recent rescript, which ordered that the sons of veterans should be compelled to serve. Martin, who had become a wanderer among churches and monasteries, was forced through information furnished by his parent to adopt the profession of a soldier. It is very probable that in after-years he may have come to see that this seeming hardship was not without some compensating benefits. The desultory kind of life into which he had fallen, however pleasant and apparently spiritual in intention, would have involved snares and dangers of its own. The three years spent in the army may be well believed to have strengthened Martin's character. The apostolic injunction must, in his ears, have sounded very specially significant. " Take thy part in suffering hardship as a good soldier of Christ Jesus. No soldier on service entangleth himself in the affairs of this life that he may please Him who enrolled him as a soldier."[1]

It was during this period that Martin performed that act of charity which, perhaps, in many minds, is most prominently associated with his name ; and which we have heard half complained of, as being so

[1] 2 Timothy ii. 3, 4 (Revised Version, *margin*).

much more widely celebrated than numberless deeds of at least equal excellence. Such semi-censure would, however, reach too far; we cannot pretend to be adequate judges of the question, what good deeds it will most profit the world to know. This particular act of Martin owes its fame, in great measure, to the circumstance that it is so well adapted to pictorial representation. But we are bound to recall it to the memory of our readers.

At Amiens, in Gaul, Martin was serving with his regiment during a winter of unusual severity. At one of the gates of the city a detachment of soldiers was besought for charity by a poor man, who was naked and shivering in the cold. The cry for alms passed unheeded; and Martin himself, who was among the number, happened at the moment, through the exercise of charity, to have nothing remaining in his purse. With his sword he cut in two the white military cloak which he was wearing, and bestowed one half upon the frozen supplicant. The appearance of Martin with his half cloak about him raised a laugh at his expense among the more thoughtless of his comrades. But there were not wanting those who felt rather ashamed of their own conduct, knowing that their own more abundant clothing could have borne such a loss more easily.

That night Martin dreamed a dream. In his sleep he saw his Lord (for whose hallowed rite of baptism he was being prepared) clad in the half cloak which he had bestowed upon the beggar. Martin thought that he was bidden to gaze carefully upon the Divine Form, and to recognise the robe which he had given away. And then it seemed to him that Jesus, addressing a host of angels standing round, distinctly said : " Martin, as yet only a catechumen, has clothed Me with this garment."

The biographer justly remarks that this is only a particular application of our Lord's own gracious declaration : "Inasmuch as ye have done it unto one of the least of these My brethren, ye have done it unto Me." Martin, he adds, while regarding the dream as an evidence of God's goodness, was by no means unduly elated, but looked upon it as a hint that it was high time for him to approach the font. Accordingly, being now in his eighteenth year, he was baptized about A.D. 334.

CHAPTER IV.

MARTIN'S WITHDRAWAL FROM THE ARMY, AND FIRST
VISIT TO ST. HILARY.

ALTHOUGH Martin would have gladly quitted his
profession immediately after his baptism, the open
avowal of Christianity did not at this period necessi-
tate such a step. By this time, even in the earlier
half of the fourth century, so considerable a number
of soldiers had become Christians, that even Non-
Christian commanders were compelled to consider
the feelings and wishes of this portion of their forces.

Julian himself, when meditating apostasy, was fully
aware of this fact; and it may have been one reason
why he temporised in the matter. Martin, though
living austerely, and resisting the temptations of his
profession, had been thoroughly popular in the army.
His immediate superior, one of the military tribunes,
begged him to stay longer, and he consented. It is
not easy to make out the exact length of Martin's
service, but he must have remained in the army
for at least three years, and probably for a longer
period.

It was under Julian,—unless Sulpicius has made a
mistake in the name and date, which is not impossible,—that Martin sought to retire. A special
expedition, for the purpose of repelling attacks from

the side of Germany, was being organised; and a fee, common on such occasions, and called a donative, was being presented to the soldiers. Martin saw that the acceptance of this fee would be naturally and reasonably understood to be a pledge of continued service. He proposed to quit the army; and, if his biographer has given us his actual words on the occasion, he implied in so doing, that his Christian profession rendered warfare unlawful. Considering that in modern times all Christians, with the exception of the Baptists and Quakers, have agreed to repudiate such a view of the requirements of the Gospel, we can hardly be surprised at the general of an army showing indignation, and taunting Martin to the effect that fear of the battle was the real motive of his conduct. To this taunt Martin replied by a declaration that he was ready to stand, on the coming day, in front cf the ranks, and, unarmed, protected only with the sign of the cross, pierce the legions of the enemy.

He was taken at his word, and kept under arrest, in order that his challenge might be tested. The seemingly eventful morrow dawned. But the enemy sent in proposals for peace, unconditionally, and Martin was allowed to leave the service.

It seems hardly possible to fix the date of the next event of any importance with which we are acquainted. Sulpicius informs us that Martin paid a visit of considerable length to Hilary, bishop of Poitiers. But if Martin really left the army as early as A.D. 336, an interval of many years is unaccounted for, inasmuch as Hilary, as we have seen, most probably did not

become bishop until about A.D. 353. The language
of Martin's biographer seems to imply that Hilary
could himself ordain ; and it does not allude to any
interval between the departure from the army and the
visit. We must be content to leave this chronological
difficulty unsolved.

Hilary, as we have already observed, appears to
have been far superior to Martin in intellectual power,
in general culture, and in knowledge of Holy Scripture. But Martin's aptitude for influencing the minds
of others must have convinced Hilary that he would
be a real acquisition to the ranks of the clergy, and
he proposed to ordain his friend and pupil as a
deacon. Martin was, however, thoroughly humble,
and declined the proposal on the ground of un-
worthiness.

Hilary did not press the point, but suggested the
more humble office of exorcist, which was then included in the ranks of the minor orders. To this
proposal Martin assented.

Soon after this appointment a dream suggested to
Martin that it was his duty to pay a visit to his own
country, and to his parents, who were still heathens.
Hilary consented, but implored Martin to return, with
a degree of impassioned entreaty, that showed how
much store he set upon his friend's companionship
and services.

Martin is said to have foretold that his journey
would involve difficulties. We are far from denying,
that it may please God to give holy men intimations
of this nature, and thus to lead them to preparation
for troubles by prayer and by the culture of a spirit of

resignation. But it is obvious that, as so often happens in biographies like that of Sulpicius, the border line between the natural and the supernatural cannot very easily be drawn. A man of the most ordinary gifts might think it highly probable that a solitary journey over difficult mountain routes, in a very unsettled state of society, could not be accomplished without considerable risk. A poet of our own century, Wordsworth, goes so far to encourage his readers to pay attention to presentiments, even when they have no such apparent basis.[1]

Whatever be thought on this point, it is right to add that Martin's alarm proved to be well founded. He lost his way among the Alps, and fell into the hands of robbers. The blow of an axe brandished over his head by one robber was warded off by another. But the band tied Martin's hands behind him, and delivered him to one of their body as his special booty. The captain took him aside to a secluded spot, and in answer to the question, " What are you !" received the reply, then recognised among believers as the proper one on all such occasions, " I am a Christian." To the further query, whether he was afraid, Martin replied that he never felt more secure, knowing, as he did, that the divine mercy would be specially accorded in trials; but that he was far more sorry for his captor, inasmuch as his profession of robbery would render him unworthy of

---

[1] In a short poem entitled "Presentiments." The wisdom of the advice is questionable. Having watched my own, and found nine out of every ten prove absolutely wrong, I have ceased to pay much regard to them.

the mercy of Christ. Martin put the Gospel before
the robber. He is said not only to have been converted, and to have set his captive free with entreaties
for his prayers, but to have told in after years the
circumstances of his conversion.

Martin, thus set at liberty, pursued his journey,
and arrived in safety at his home, though he believed
that in passing Milan, Satan, arrayed in human form,
announced to him his determined hostility. At the
reply, " The Lord is my helper, and I will not fear
what man doeth unto me," the enemy vanished.

It is not uncommon, both in matters temporal and
spiritual, to find that the links of affection are closer
and more potent between the minds of son and
mother than of son and father. In the instance of
Anthusa and Chrysostom, of Monica and Augustine,
it was the mother who was mainly instrumental in
the conversion of the son. In the case of Martin
the order was reversed. He converted his mother,
but his father remained a pagan. His mother was,
however, by no means his only convert in the
district.

Martin met with opposition in Illyricum, not only
from pagan unbelievers, but also from Arians.
Arianism was especially strong in that region, and it
had infected the minds of the clergy. His almost
solitary championship of the Catholic faith led to his
being publicly scourged and expelled from the country.
Having heard of the banishment of his friend Hilary
and the generally disturbed state of Gaul, Martin
determined to betake himself to Italy, and began to
found a monastic institution at Milan. But Arianism

pursued him thither. Auxentius, the bishop of the see, with whom Hilary had a severe contest, plotted against Martin (as both Sozomen and Severus inform us), and, after greatly harassing him, drove him from the city. This second expulsion from the haunts of men convinced Martin that a temporary retirement would be wise. He was fortunate in finding a presbyter of most excellent character, who sympathised with him, and the two friends retired to a small island in the Mediterranean. This island, of which the modern name Gallinare is but slightly altered from its ancient one Gallinaria, lies off the coast line known as the Riviera, not far from the town of Albenga.

The food of the two exiles consisted simply of herbs. Martin partook of some hellebore, and felt himself virtually poisoned by it. We say *virtually* because modern investigation declares that this plant used in moderation is, though not nutritious, in some cases medicinal.[1] Here, again, we find ourselves on the border-line between the natural and the supernatural. Unquestionably He who enabled Elisha of old to render the poisonous wild gourds harmless may have in like manner undone the bad effects of hellebore on the frame of Martin. But extraordinary answers to prayer on behalf of the sick are of

---

[1] It is commonly asserted that Paracelsus, who flourished at the epoch of the Reformation, was the first to employ as medicines substances commonly known as poisons, and actually such if taken in excess, beginning with laudanum. In our own day iodine and even strychnine are thus used. Many readers will remember Paracelsus as the hero of Mr. Browning's drama.

constant occurrence in our own and in old times. All that we can say in this case is that Martin felt himself to be alarmingly ill, and believed that he was at the point of death. He prayed earnestly, and a sudden freedom from pain with complete recovery was granted. These events in Martin's life, from the visit to his parents to the conclusion of the retirement in Gallinaria, can be fixed with tolerable precision. They must have occurred between A.D. 356–360.

CHAPTER V.

MARTIN RETURNS TO GAUL AND FOUNDS A MONASTERY NEAR POITIERS.

SOON after his recovery from this attack, Martin heard, to his great satisfaction, that his friend and instructor Hilary had obtained permission from the Emperor to return to his see. Martin tried to effect a junction with the bishop of Poitiers on his homeward journey, and with this intention set out for Rome. But he was too late, as Hilary had already gone northward: nor did these allies meet until Martin, following in the tracks of Hilary, found the latter already re-settled at Poitiers. On the second occasion, as on that of his first visit, Martin was warmly welcomed. Being, however, bent upon monastic life, Martin retired to a spot now known as Lugugé (a contracted form of its ancient name Locociagum), some five miles distant from Poitiers.

The way in which we here regard the narratives concerning miracles has already been indicated. We trust that our readers will pardon another digression which seems to rise naturally out of our subject. Martin is, at the point we have now reached, beginning to undertake the conversion of the large tracts of Gaul which were still heathen, as a monk and an ascetic. For fairness sake it seems proper to state

our sentiments on that point also. Let it be premised that by the ascetic principle we understand a
voluntary self-denial of something that is lawful in
itself, for the sake of greater devotedness to the
service of God.

Now, no candid reader of the Bible can possibly
deny that asceticism has a real place in its pages, and
receives a divine recognition. The Mosaic dispensation has its own rules concerning the Nazarites, as
we may see by reference to the sixth chapter of the
book of Numbers. A very devout commentator, in
whom the Protestant element is strongly marked,[1]
and who calls attention to the contrast of Nazaritic
rules in details with those of Mediæval Christendom,
yet writes concerning this institution as follows:—
"The Lord Himself set apart Samson and John
the Baptist before their birth to be Nazarites all
their days: Samuel was devoted by his mother
to be a perpetual Nazarite, when he was 'asked
of the Lord,' and the family of the Rechabites
were a sort of Nazarites from one generation to another, by the injunction of Jonadab their progenitor.
. . . . Among the distinguishing favours which God
conferred on Israel, it is stated, 'that He raised up of
their young men for Nazarites,' whence we may infer
that their prayers, examples, and instructions were
considered as a public blessing." In the Speaker's
Commentary on the same chapter, the spirit of
Nazaritism is justly described as "that zeal for God
which, not content with observing what is obligatory,

[1] The Rev. Thomas Scott.

seeks for higher and stricter modes of self-dedication." The list of Nazarites must include, in the spirit if not in the letter, the great prophets Elijah and Elisha. We also know how St. Paul took upon himself for a few days the formal vows of a Nazarite.

Christian sorrow may be a lower thing than Christian joy ; but for us, being what we are, the sorrow seems the more attainable, the joy running so great a risk of becoming of the earth, earthy,—perhaps even carnal. During this life the sorrow bears the higher hand. In the words of a great master of fiction, "There is something in melancholy feelings more natural to an imperfect and suffering state than in those of gaiety, and when they are brought into collision the former seldom fail to triumph. If a funeral-train and wedding-procession were to meet unexpectedly, it will readily be allowed that the mirth of the last would be speedily merged in the gloom of the other."[1] In like manner it may be said that abstractedly the non-ascetic life, which is that of the angels and of unfallen man, is the higher ; but it may be that this does not hold good for the sons of Adam since the fall.

We cannot pause to enter into a detailed comparison of these two states of life. Beyond question, it is only the few who can be fitted for asceticism. Consequently, when attempted on a large scale, and for any length of time, it breaks down, and leads to terrible failure and evil. "The accumulated wealth and idleness of the innumerable religious orders"[2]

---

[1] Sir Walter Scott, "Peveril of the Peak," chap. iv.
[2] "John Inglesant," vol. ii., chap. i. (London, 1882.)

is justly named as one of the causes of the temporal
ruin of the Italy of the sixteenth and seventeenth
centuries; and it is said in the present day to be one
of the great difficulties in the way of the improvement
of Sicily.

Nevertheless, under both the old and new dispensa-
tions, the ascetic life has done a great work. Its minis-
trations have proved peculiarly grand where ordinary
ones are but too apt to fail in the correction of the
rich and great.   It is an ascetic who rebukes Ahab;
it is an ascetic who reproves Herod Antipas; it is an
ascetic who preaches unwelcome truth before a Felix
and an Agrippa.

In our own day thinkers, who are certainly not
prejudiced in favour of asceticism, acknowledge
how much we owe to it in the ages that have
passed away.   The candid bishop of Winchester,
Dr. Harold Browne, acknowledges monasticism as
one of those elements without which he does not
see how Christianity could have traversed the middle
ages.   Dean Milman speaks most truly of the calm
example of the domestic virtues being of "ines-
timable value as spreading around the parsonage an
atmosphere of peace and happiness, and offering a
living lesson on the blessings of conjugal fidelity."
But he adds no less forcibly, that "such Christianity
would have made no impression, even if it could
have existed, on a people who still retained something of their Teutonic severity of manners, and
required something more imposing,—a sterner and
more manifest self-denial,—to keep up their religious
veneration.   The detachment of the clergy from all

P

earthly ties left them at once more unremittingly
devoted to their unsettled life as missionaries ; more
ready to encounter the perils of this wild age ; while
at the same time the rude minds of the people were
more struck by their unusual habits, by the strength
of character shown in their labours, their mortifica-
tions, their fastings, and perpetual religious services."[1]

Professor Wace, in an admirable but brief article
in "Good Words," in speaking of St. Antony, writes
as follows :—"As to the monastic life itself, even if
this extreme form, before its adoption at that time by
men naturally inclined for it, be adversely criticised,
it would demand serious consideration, whether, in
a state of society steeped in corruption to an extent
which, probably, we can none of us realise, some
vehement revolt of this kind against the ordinary life
of the world was not equally imperative and service-
able. *It was, perhaps, the most conspicuous and influential factor in Christian life at the time.*"[2]

And a Presbyterian, Dr. A. K. H. Boyd, of St.
Andrews, in recounting the history of the conversion
of Scotland to Christianity, writes as follows, after
telling how the secular organisation had been unsuc-
cessful :—"Another organisation came in God's
Providence ; and the monastic rule succeeded where

[1] "Latin Christianity," book iv., chap. iii.
[2] "Good Words," p. 684, 1878, art. "Controversy of St.
Athanasius with Arianism." This excellent paper has a real connexion with the life of St. Hilary as well as that of St. Martin.
A study of it would throw much light on some previous parts
of this little volume, *e.g.*, the chapter headed "Questions at
Issue."

the secular had failed. Only the utmost prejudice, founding on the utmost ignorance, will deny the good work done by monasteries and a' monastic clergy in their day of purity, energy, and self-devotion; or will deny that they were admirably fitted to do the work they did. The Christian Church needed not only dissemination, but also strong centres. . . . And the monks did good work in divers ways. They spread a zone of cultivated land around them, reclaimed from the morass and the forest. . . . Amid the terrible insecurity of life, and the utter disregard of right and wrong, which we can discern to have been characteristics of heathenism, here was comparative security, here were truth and righteousness. The monasteries were places of education ; they were schools,—the only schools known for many a day. And, while printing was yet unknown, here a constant work went on of multiplying copies of Holy Scripture; but for which the Bible might almost have perished. Nor need we forget, we [Presbyterians] who miss it so sadly, the ever-recurring hour of prayer and praise ; the Psalms, notably, from beginning to end, kept familiar, as they are to very few of us."[1]

A great misfortune, revealing a sad state of spiritual declension, befell God's ancient people. There came an epoch when religion was placed before them, first in an ascetic, and then in a non-ascetic form. If they could have sympathised with either kind of devotion, all might have been well, though happiest would have been they who could have appreciated

---

[1] "St. Giles's Lectures," first series, pp. 38, 39.

each in turn. They rejected both. "John came neither eating nor drinking, and they say he hath a devil. • The Son of Man came eating and drinking, and they say, Behold a gluttonous man and a wine-bibber, a friend of publicans and sinners." "But wisdom is justified of her children."[1] It may not be amiss for us to think over the question, how far we are among the children of the true wisdom, if we find ourselves unable to enter into modes of thought and action which have received the sublime and emphatic sanction of such authority.

The rule adopted by Martin for his monastic establishment was doomed to succumb, in after years, to the still more popular, perhaps more wise and practical, rule of St. Benedict. But it was by means of his monastery, both before and after his elevation to the episcopate, that Martin did so much for the conversion of Gaul to Christianity, and stamped his name upon the heart and imagination of the land of his adoption, and of many countries beyond its limits.

[1] St. Matt. xl. 18, 19; St. Luke vii. 35. The reading in St. Matthew, "And wisdom is justified by her works," adopted in the Revised Version, adds force to the general lesson conveyed.

CHAPTER VI.

MARTIN BECOMES BISHOP OF TOURS.

For eleven years, as nearly as we are able to calculate, Martin, gathering around him a company of monks into whom he infused a large portion of his own energy, continued to evangelise the country at large, more especially the district around his monastery at Lugugé. That it may have pleased the Almighty to aid his endeavours by some extraordinary answers to prayer, we have already admitted. Each particular instance must stand upon its own evidence. Unfortunately Martin's biographer, Sulpicius, displays no perception of the meaning of the word evidence. His one argument is that our Lord promised that His disciples should work miracles; and that, consequently, if we disbelieve the narratives of any of the miracles ascribed to the evangeliser of Gaul, we are guilty of disbelief in the words of Christ Himself. Such a principle would involve a necessity of belief in the report of every miracle alleged to have been wrought by any sincere Christian.

Some of the narratives present singular features. Thus, for example, it is strange to read how Martin recalled to life the servant of a man of distinction, named Lupicinus. The servant had hung himself, and the biographer does not say a passing word upon

any idea of blame being attached to suicide : though
of course it is possible that the poor man may have
acted under the pressure of temporary insanity.
Generally, however, the exertion of any supernatural
power recorded of Martin is connected with some
work of mercy. In one instance, his spiritual insight
was exerted to repress superstition. Veneration was
being exhibited at the shrine of a supposed saint.
Martin was unconvinced of the genuineness of the
claim, and is said to have compelled the spirit of the
deceased to confess that he had been a robber who
was executed for his crimes.

At length the impression made upon the public
mind by Martin convinced the Christians of the parts
around that he ought to be elevated to the episcopate.
The difficulty concerning the office of a bishop lies,
not in the evidence for its apostolic origin, which will
bear ample investigation, but in its practical working.
The gifts required for the proper discharge of the
office are so numerous and varied, the temptations
incident to it are so grave and so subtle, that to find
men fit for the position has ever been, and must ever
be, one of the gravest of all practical problems. On
this point it would be easy to bring together evidence
from every age, after the fire of persecution had
passed away. It is not merely the satirists from
outside who use hard language concerning the ambition of candidates for the office and the faults of
the order considered as a class ; grave historians and
biographers are quite as emphatic, and the judgment
is not confined to any part of Christendom nor to
any school of thought. Within the last year an

American bishop of what is called the Evangelical school has left it on record that, if men knew the perils of the post, they would flee and hide themselves when a see became vacant, in order that they might not be chosen : and we are told by a Roman Catholic writer of ultramontane views, the late Father Faber, "that an eminent spiritual writer has remarked that the elevation to the episcopate has in most instances been found to be the cause of relaxed strictness and mortification," at any rate during the first year of the episcopate.

That in Martin's age the office was often sought in an ambitious and worldly spirit seems clear enough. But there were also many who shrunk from it, and it was obvious that Martin, who had been unwilling to be ordained deacon, would prove far more unwilling to take upon himself the responsibility of being enrolled among the chief rulers of the · Church. The see of Tours had, however, become vacant, and the determination of a large number of church-people to have Martin for its bishop was most manifest. One great cause of perplexity remained, namely, How was the monk to be allured from his monastery? It was, we fear, only too much in accordance with the current ideas upon such matters that recourse was had to what is called a pious stratagem. A citizen of Tours, named Ruricius, pretending that his wife was ill, implored Martin to come and see her. Arrangements had been made for bands of citizens to be on the route, and the visitor arrived under something like a virtual guard.   .

On his arrival Martin found a large crowd, which was greatly increased by contingents of voters from neighbouring cities. The clergy and laity were almost unanimous in demanding his election. There were, however, a few dissentients, especially among the bishops. They objected to his general appearance as despicable, to his sordid vestments, and his unkempt hair. But the current of feeling was too strong to be resisted, though one bishop, named Defensor, continued to stand out. On the day appointed for the election the presbyter whose turn it was to say the service failed to reach the church in time, in consequence of the pressure of the crowd. Another took up a Psalter and read out the first verse at which he chanced to open the book. It was the second verse of the eighth Psalm, which in our Authorised Version stands as follows :—" Out of the mouth of babes and sucklings hast thou ordained strength, because of thine enemies, that thou mightest still the enemy and the avenger." The Latin version known as the Vulgate has the same rendering ; but in the translation then used in Gaul, probably the one known as the Old Italic (*Vetus Itala*), the last words of this verse ran thus, "ut destruas inimicum et *defensorem*." The aptness of the quotation delighted the friends of Martin. It was quite in accordance with the spirit of the age, that it was regarded as a divine inspiration, and it seems to have confounded the opponents of the proposed candidate, as much as it elevated the spirit of his supporters. A loud shout was raised. Opposition thenceforth ceased and Martin was duly consecrated bishop of Tours. Tours, as some perhaps may remember, was long regarded as the capital of the province of Touraine. It lies on that rapid river, the Loire, which washes Orleans, Bourges, and other important cities. Its ecclesiastical glories were sadly shattered in the great French revolution of 1789; but it is still a place of importance, and contains some 28,000 people.

There were at this time some ten or eleven sees in Gaul, and it may surprise the reader to find that so large a portion of the country remained pagan. But these episcopal seats lay mostly in the south and south-eastern district, so that Tours was one of the most central. Moreover, according to the custom prevalent in most parts of Christendom, they were all placed in cities. Now, the very word which has just been employed, *pagan*, simply means, as is well known, a countryman; and its secondary sense of non-Christian arose from the circumstance that the people in country villages were the last to be reached by the gospel-message.

To assert that Martin possessed all the gifts needed for a complete discharge of the duties of the episcopate would be an over-statement. He was not learned, and could not possibly have achieved the task wrought by his friend Hilary. His monastic rules, unlike those of the Benedictine order, made scarcely any provision for the cultivation of learning; excepting that the younger members of the order were taught to cultivate the art of transcribing. This was indeed no light matter for posterity, when we consider the number of valuable books which must otherwise have perished in the ages before printing was discovered. But copying, though subsidiary to learning, did not necessarily make men scholars.

Neither can it be said, that the famous bishop of Tours displayed any extraordinary powers in council with his brother bishops as regards the general government of the church. This is a point which must come before us in a subsequent chapter.

But in the often-quoted words of the Roman poet " we cannot all of us accomplish everything" (*non omnia possumus omnes*). Only a few, even among the rulers of the church, come in after years to be recognised among its doctors. Nor, indeed, is it to be desired. There are times and places where an immediate work and direct influence over the minds of men and women are of more value than any amount of learning. Such influence Martin certainly possessed, at any rate among the great mass of those with whom he was brought in contact. He could not have done the work of Hilary; but neither could Hilary have done that of Martin.

Gifted now with the authority of his office and with the *prestige* (if we may use the word in a good sense) which always accompanies it, Martin commenced fresh operations upon the paganism of Gaul. He built a new monastery about two miles out of Tours. His zeal and the charm of his personality brought together a great number of disciples. Although the discipline was severely ascetic—the usual dress being of camel's skin, and wine only allowed to the infirm,— yet many of noble origin, trained in very different habits, joined the community. The fame of this

monastery was soon spread abroad, and the spirit of
endurance and of humility there fostered induced the
electors to other vacant sees to seek their bishops
from this quarter.

The journeys of Martin in Gaul during his episcopate seem to have been tolerably extensive; and we
hear of him as far north as Paris. They were marked,
according to Severus, by a great number of miraculous attestations in the way of relief given to the
sick and leprous and especially to the possessed. It
must not, however, be forgotten that by this time the
power of the state, which for three centuries had at
intervals so cruelly persecuted the Christians, was now
engaged upon the opposite side. Indeed the Emperor
Constantius had used the authority of the crown
against heathenism to an extent which some eminent
modern historians (as, for example, Döllinger and De
Broglie) condemn as certainly, to say the least, unwise.
That Martin and other Christian teachers of his day
freely made use of the advantages thus accorded to
them in the demolition of pagan temples and the conse-
quent cessation of many pagan rites is undeniable: and
appeals on the part of the heathen to the imperial courts
seem to have met with but small success. One French
historian, Sismondi, who, though most generous to
opponents of the later ages, is generally unjust to the
early and to the mediæval church, dwells upon this
feature of the case in a hostile tone. But even
Sismondi is compelled to grant that such persecution
as was waged against heathenism in Gaul never
touched the persons of its adherents. What might
have happened if those adherents had resisted we

cannot tell.   The case was never tried.   Heathenism,
as all historians (including Sismondi) grant, produced no martyrs.   The contrast in this respect
with the religion of the Cross is, indeed, most truly
significant.

CHAPTER VII.

MARTIN AND THE AUTHORITIES OF THE STATE.

IN speaking of the points of contrast between the career of Martin and his friend Hilary one has been omitted. It is that which is suggested by the title of the present chapter.

Both of these prelates, as, indeed, was almost inevitable in those times, came across the rulers of the state. But, whereas the position of Hilary in relation to the imperial authorities was constantly one of opposition, that of Martin was for the most part very much the reverse. He was courted by an emperor, and humbly waited upon by an empress. For all time this relation has been found one of greater trial than that of hostility. The old fable is often realised : the keen blast of persecution makes the traveller fold the cloak of principle more closely around him ; but the sun of favour may tempt him to release his clasps, and at length to throw his mantle on one side.

The emperor with whom Hilary was most concerned was, as we have seen, Constantius. In the case of Martin it was Maximus. Now, Maximus was a usurper. Still it must be remembered that such a title did not carry, and ought not to carry, with it the amount of stigma which may be justly associated

with it in other times and climes. The Roman
empire was itself based on usurpation. Augustus was
a usurper, and some of the best among his successors
(as, for example, Vespasian) were usurpers. Vespasian
had reached a position, as a successful general, which
made his friends urge upon him that no choice was
left; that it would not be believed that he had no
designs upon the purple, and that he must either seize
it or he would probably be put to death.

Something similar to this had, according to his own
account, happened to Maximus. About A.D. 368,
perhaps a little later, he had been sent to Britain as
general. There he remained several years; but discontent spread among his troops, not through any
fault of Maximus, but in consequence of the bad
judgment of the Emperor Gratian. Gratian was so
partial to foreign barbarians, that his promotions
naturally provoked the soldiery. A revolt broke out,
and its result was the overthrow of Gratian and the
accession of Maximus to imperial power. Gratian,
after having been defeated by Maximus near Paris,
was slain not far from Lyons when attempting to
fly to Italy. The reigning sovereigns, Theodosius
and Valentinian, the brothers of Gratian, agreed to
recognise Maximus as emperor in Gaul, Spain, and
Britain. His reign lasted five years, from A.D. 383–
388 ; and it was during these years that Maximus and
Martin met.

Maximus had shortly before his elevation become
a Christian. We have no reason to question the sincerity of his conversion, though the day when such a
step involved a political risk was certainly gone by.

On the general question, however, of his conduct towards Gratian, it is not easy to decide how much of blame is due to Maximus.[1] That the troops virtually forced him to accept the crown seems undeniable. But the question arises whether he had himself fomented the disaffection of the soldiers. And here the evidence is conflicting. One authority, Zosimus,[2] says that Maximus had encouraged the discontent, while another, Orosius, denies it. The circumstance that Orosius was a Christian and Zosimus a pagan may beget a suspicion of partiality on either side. Nor can we feel that we are entitled to appeal to the authority of Sulpicius Severus as that of an arbiter between these adversaries. He is decidedly favourable to Maximus, entitling him "a man who would have deserved every possible eulogy, if it had been in his power to refuse the diadem unlawfully forced upon him, or to abstain from civil war." But Sulpicius is almost sure to be partial to any one who looked up to Martin. Possibly Maximus may have been sincere for a time; but the conclusion of his career, his determination to add Italy to his dominions, does not look like the course of the consistent penitent which he claimed to be. This problem must be left to the judgment of the reader. It is high time

[1] See art. Maximus, Magnus Clemens, in Smith's "Dictionary of Greek and Roman Biography."

[2] In 1830 Louis-Philippe had to choose between acceptance of the power resigned by Charles X. and a second and final exile from France. As in the case of Maximus, the question has been mooted, "Had the Duke of Orleans in any wise fostered the disturbances by which he profited?" Problems of a similar nature do thus occasionally recur in history.

for us to recount the relations of the emperor with Martin.

Maximus, on his recognition as Augustus and sole emperor in the provinces above named, took up his residence at the ancient city of Trèves. His success had been so rapid and brilliant that a crowd of courtiers soon gathered around him. Sulpicius (in whose pages the episcopate as a body does not come off well) declares that several bishops were prominent among these courtiers, and displayed the greatest subservience. Martin alone preserved apostolic dignity. Even in his entreaties that the lives of certain captives might be spared, his attitude was more that of a man ordering another to do what was right than of one who is suing for a favour. Nor, though frequently invited, would he for some time come as a guest to the imperial banquets, alleging, as his reason, "that he could not share the meals of one who had deprived one emperor (Valentinian) of his kingdom and another (Gratian) of his life." Maximus, in reply, made the excuses to which reference has already been made, namely, that empire had been forced upon him; and Martin at length consented to be his guest.

That this concession was a subject of great rejoicing to Maximus need not be doubted. It interested both the lower and the higher promptings of his ambition; for such had become by this time the influence of Martin that his sanction was a fresh accession of strength to any civil ruler, and Maximus may have been quite sincere in his wish to prove to himself that he had, as he maintained, been simply following the leadings of God's providence.

An incident at the imperial banquet has been often told. Maximus, when a goblet of wine was brought to him by an attendant, ordered that it should be first taken to the holy bishop, who was his guest. The emperor expected that he would enjoy the satisfaction of receiving the vessel from the hands of Martin. But the bishop, having drunk from it, handed the goblet to the presbyter who was acting as his attendant chaplain, holding him to be the next in dignity. How this action would have been regarded on the part of other prelates may be a question. It was certainly unusual, and had not, Sulpicius tells us, been ventured upon by any other bishop at the feast of imperial authorities of the lowest rank. As it was, it met with admiring approbation from the emperor and all his guests.

The empress, the wife of Maximus, surpassed her husband in admiration of the Bishop of Tours. In company with the emperor, she listened to Martin's conversation concerning the glories of heaven, and the world present and future. At length she obtained leave to offer Martin a banquet, which she had prepared with her own hands, and at which she alone ministered to him as a servant. At its conclusion the empress collected the crumbs and fragments of Martin's repast as a meal for her own consumption. Sulpicius considers that some apology may be requisite for Martin's conduct in this instance. Accordingly, he calls attention to the circumstances that the bishop was at this time a man of seventy, that the princess was no longer young, and was acting with the full consent of her husband. He adds that the

Q

objects with which Martin paid this and other visits to the palace were the liberation of prisoners, the recall of the banished from exile, and the restoration to others of property which had been confiscated.[1]

[1] We have no certain information respecting the name of this empress; but some authors have tried to make out that she was named Helena, and was a daughter of a wealthy nobleman called Eudda, who resided at Caersegont (now Caernarvon) in Wales.

CHAPTER VIII.

MARTIN AND CIVIL RULERS, *cont.*—THE CASE OF PRISCILLIAN.

THE relations between Martin and Maximus were destined to complications far greater than anything arising out of questions of the etiquette proper to be obšerved in banquets, or the forgiveness of adversaries who had been mixed up with the contests between rival claimants for the diadem. This emperor has the unenviable distinction of being the first sovereign who put a heretic to death. It is right to observe that Maximus maintained that the persons accused had been bad subjects, and had been guilty of witchcraft and of grievous immoralities. This was not, however, the general impression produced upon the minds of bystanders. Priscillian—such was the name of the sufferer—was generally supposed to have been put to death for his opinions.

An examination of details might easily lead us away into two lengthy digressions ; one on the precise nature of the errors of Priscillian, and another on the general question of toleration. Happily for the reader, our limits forbid long wanderings. But a few words on each point are absolutely required.

It is somewhat singular that both judge and victim, Maximus and Priscillian, were natives of Spain.

Q 2

Priscillian was superior to the emperor in the matter of origin, being of a noble family, whereas that of Maximus was obscure. Further, Priscillian was one of a class of men who, if they do take a wrong turn, are all the more dangerous; because, even by the admission of their keenest opponents, they are really endowed with many high and valuable gifts. He was not only noble and rich, but was also truly learned, quick in power of argument, keen, and eloquent. He was able to endure fast and vigil, and free from all rapacity and from the indulgence which his wealth might suggest. At the same time he was accused of inordinate vanity, and was believed, whether truly or not, to have practised magical arts from his infancy.

Priscillianism is represented to us as a mixture of Manichæism and Gnosticism. A discussion on Manichæism would come in more fitly in a life of St. Augustine, inasmuch as that great doctor of the Church was for eight years entangled in its meshes. It must suffice to say that this system attacks the very foundation of all religion, both natural and revealed. For it teaches that there is not one God, but two principles,—a principle of good and a principle of evil, ever contending against each other. The blessings of life are attributable to the good principle, the evils to its rival. This theory is not without a certain seductiveness to the natural temper and reason of fallen man. It had long been popular in the East, and derives support, to say the least, from the Zendavesta, the collection of books esteemed sacred by the ancient Persians. In our own day, in

England it fascinated for a time James Mill, the father of John Stuart Mill, and he wondered that it was not revived.

Gnosticism is a much more complex theme. After all the labours of Dr. Burton, Dean Mansel, and Bishop Lightfoot in England; of Neander, Möhler,   . Gieseler, and numbers more in Germany, many questions concerning its nature and origin still remain unanswered. In this place we can only say that the Gnostics at least claimed to be a kind of Christians, but that they tried to form an intellectual and spiritual aristocracy essentially alien to its spirit. Though less directly antagonistic in theory to the faith than the Manichæans, they resembled them in their attempts to solve the mystery of the existence of evil, and to reconcile its presence with the creation of the universe by God. They arrived at the conclusion that matter was the abode of evil. This conclusion — led to two opposite ways of meeting the difficulty in practice. Some Gnostics took up a severely ascetic line. Others, finding the impossibility of carrying out asceticism, so as to avoid all contact with matter, resolved to regard such difficulties as a matter of indifference, and rushed into the most reckless licentiousness. A connexion with magical practices seems to have been common. Hence, apparently, the importance of the burning of those books on curious arts at Ephesus, as recorded in the Acts of the Apostles (xix. 19).

According to Sulpicius, Gnosticism had first been introduced into Spain, within the lifetime of Martin, by an Egyptian named Mark, a native of Memphis, the ancient capital of that land, now included in the bounds of Cairo.

St. Augustine has said that the leading heretics have all been great men, and he is probably right. High endowments have been sadly perverted; " the things which should have been for their wealth be-came unto them an occasion of falling." In the case of Priscillianism an element of aid came in which must not wholly be passed by in silence.

In the Book which, in addition to its highest and holiest characteristics, sets before us a whole gallery of portraits which illustrate the capacities of our fallen nature, we have a long series of saintly women. Miriam, Ruth, Deborah, Hannah, the Queen of Sheba, may be named as among specimens of pre-Christian times. The pages of the New Testament are, as might be expected, still richer : there we meet with Elizabeth, Anna, Dorcas, the holy band which accompanied our Lord Himself and ministered to Him of their substance,—those who were, as has been often noted, "the last at the Cross and the first at the sepulchre."

But a Latin proverb reminds us that the corruption of that which is most excellent falls naturally into the opposite extreme.[1] If the feminine temperament be more inclined to piety than the masculine ; if among specimens of purely human saintliness it is impossible to name one higher than the Virgin Mother of the Lord, no less true it is that the same elements of character, when once perverted, become sometimes

---

[1] "Corruptio optimi pessima."

more mischievous and terrible than even those of wicked men. An Ahab and a Herod Antipas leave on the mind a fainter impression of guilty power than their partners in crime—Jezebel and Herodias.

Uninspired literature presents a similar picture. Greek legends, which tell of an Andromache, a Penelope, an Antigone, portray for us also the lineaments of a Phædra and a Clytemnestra. And the one limner who has drawn a set of female portraits unequalled in the whole realm of letters, side by side with Portia, Cordelia, Imogen, Desdemona, Queen Catherine, and so many more types of varied beauty of mind, has also left us the awe-inspiring features of Lady Macbeth and of Regan and Goneril. The annals of actual history will be found to sanction such a representation of the excellences and the perils of womanhood.

Consequently, we must not be surprised if in the pages of that Church history, which beyond any other earthly record is gemmed and studded with the names of noble and devoted women, we meet with phases of an opposite description. Even in apostolic times false teachers could find silly and immoral women, whom they were able to lead captive and enthral (2 Tim. iii. 6). Within the first five centuries, without coming down later, we find women of every rank in society prominent in the records, so terrible, yet so glorious, of martyrdom. There are virgin martyrs, such as St. Lucy and Blandina ; there are matrons, such as Saints Perpetua and Felicitas ; there are also mothers to whom has been largely due, under God, the formation of the character of their sons—sons, such as a Chrysostom and an Augustine, who might well say to their Maker with the Psalmist: "I am Thy servant, *and the son of Thine handmaid.*" Of their influence in exalted station some idea may be formed from the saying, that for the conversion of a kingdom from heathenism to Christianity three things were commonly found requisite: a national calamity, a monk, and a princess. Nor must we forget the honourable part often played by them in mollifying the wrath of an offended father or husband, for this is a line of conduct which is absent from many non-Christian religions. Mohammedan history only mentions one instance of such an interference,—that of Zobeide, wife of the famous Caliph Haroun-al-Raschid. Of the energetic action of nuns, and of great ladies also on behalf of champions of the faith, it is almost unnecessary to speak, so patent is it on the very face of ecclesiastical history. But though the actions of the great have gained the accidental glory which is blazoned, so to speak, in the heraldry of the Church's annals, we cannot doubt but that thousands of their lowlier sisters have been fully their equals in everything but celebrity.

Nevertheless, there were cases in which feminine countenance and aid were accorded to heretics. Among teachers of error who were conspicuously supported in this way must be mentioned Arius and Priscillian. Arius, at the commencement of his career, is said to have carried away with him into heretical doctrines as many as seven hundred nuns.[1]

---

[1] Epiphanius, "Hæreses," § 69, cited by Cardinal Newman in "Historical Sketches," p. 379.

Priscillian enjoyed much support from the women of Spain.

The new heresiarch had other strong points in his favour. He was, as has been said, a man of wealth and good social position. Nor does there seem at first to have been anything against his character. This need not surprise us. There are men who have overcome, there are men who have hardly ever felt the temptations of Belial and Mammon. Their difficulty may have lain in the region of the intellect and will. The love of singularity; the fascination of becoming a leader of society; the satisfaction of gathering a party of adherents; the love of power and of fame; these and such like allurements often plead strongly with tempers naturally pure and noble, and lead them into many perils. Whatever error such men teach is, of course, far more dangerous to those around than the heresy of the avowedly worldly and immoral; but it does not thereby cease to be false. Pelagianism is none the less a deadly error, because St. Augustine could describe his great opponent as being not only most acute, but "illustriously Christian," and his friends as " men of pure life and praiseworthy character."[1]

From its first appearance in Spain, the form of Gnosticism taught by Priscillian was treated with much severity by those in authority, whether civil or ecclesiastical. A Spanish bishop, by name Ithacius, came forward as a leading opponent of the new heresy. Ithacius is mentioned with honour by a

---

[1] In his tractate, "De Peccatorum Meritis et Remissione," tom. x., pp. 73, 74, in the Benedictine edition.

famous episcopal historian of later date,—Isidore of Seville; but he is not a favourite with Martin's biographer, Sulpicius. This is not wonderful, inasmuch as Ithacius was by no means in full sympathy with the work and character of Martin; and on one occasion went to the extreme length of insinuating a mistaken charge of heresy against the Bishop of Tours. But Priscillian also had his friends in the episcopate; and these, despite the condemnation uttered by a local council, procured his consecration to a see then vacant—that of Avila. This small city in Old Castile still retains its ancient name. It was destined to become famous as the birth-place, in A.D. 1515, of one who is assuredly in the highest rank among female authors, the most remarkable woman whom the Church of Rome has ever canonized —St. Teresa.

The opponents of Priscillian, on hearing of this step, had recourse to the civil power. It is difficult to see how, while the world endures, the Church and State can avoid at times acting in conjunction in a given crisis, or else coming into collision. They often act in conjunction, because both are interested in the preservation of peace and order; both are likely to encourage some kind of education; both are deeply concerned with the arrangement of two of the greatest bonds of civilized society; that is to say, with property and marriage. They often come into collision, because the special authorities of each may differ profoundly on the questions whether order may be too deeply purchased by stagnation; how far property may be wisely bestowed on the support of art and science, of philanthropy and piety ; how far national education ought to be based upon the tenets of religion, natural or revealed ; and how far marriage is to be regarded as a civil and even dissoluble contract. That when the age of heathen persecution had passed away the Church did obtain, and did sometimes even seek, aid from the civil power, is undeniable. State penalties were employed against the Donatists ; and Augustine approved it, though it is fair to say that the coercion stopped short of capital punishment. What degree of alliance and co-partnership is in such matters right and desirable has been a fertile subject of controversy, which is by no means yet extinct. There has been the view taken by emperors like Constantine and Theodosius ; the Hildebrandine view, which would make the State simply the Church's policeman—a view by no means confined to lands beyond the Alps and those controlled by papal organisations ; and the theories set forth in England by Hooker and by Warburton, by Coleridge and Gladstone, by Arnold and Macaulay, to say nothing of works published in other parts of Britain, or in Europe and America. That we are far from having seen the end of controversy on this fertile theme is evident from the merest glance at passing events ; and if theory rather than direct action be demanded, it is enough to refer to the powerful and (in many passages) startling work of a living English judge, Mr. Justice Stephen, on " Liberty, Equality, and Fraternity."[1]

---

[1] London, 1873.

Closely intertwined with this most thorny problem
comes the difficulty which emerged so forcibly in the
case of Priscillian, the question of toleration,—a
question which both in theory and in practice has
been ever found in the past, and still remains in our
own day, one of the most profoundly difficult which
can engage the attention of civilized society.

To some minds it would appear an easy solution
of this problem to say : "Let us tolerate everything in
the way of opinion." But this theory meets with a
speedy check. Thus, for example, the British rulers
of Hindostan found a sect who held the opinion that
it was lawful, and even religiously praiseworthy, to
decoy a traveller into their company, strangle him,
and throw his corpse into a grave which had been
previously prepared. Not only did our Anglo-Indian
statesmen effectually put down this sect (known as the
Thugs), in practice, but we believe that even a Brahmin
—and there were Brahmins among the Thugs—would
have found that his high caste did not protect him
from something very like persecution if he publicly
avowed the doctrines which he held. In short, as Mr.
Froude has well expressed it, "You cannot tolerate
those who will not tolerate you."

The circle is then somewhat narrowed. Men
may next, however, proceed to say: "Let us tolerate both in theory and practice whatever is not
decidedly against the moral law." But the difficulty
is not hereby solved. Polygamy, however much at
variance with the rule of Christ's Church, cannot be
pronounced to be a distinct breach of the moral law.
Yet, inasmuch as it overthrows the entire framework

of that modern civilisation which has been raised upon a basis of Christian ideas, the Government of the United States has found the toleration of Mormonism to be in practice all but impossible.

It is not easy to mention a single treatise which can be said to approximate to a satisfactory treatment of the question. This is not from lack of authors, or of ability on the part of those who have discussed the subject. Bishop Jeremy Taylor, John Locke, Coleridge, J. S. Mill, and Mr. Justice Stephen have all handled the problem. But which of them has succeeded? Bishop Taylor draws a line at the holding of the Apostles' Creed, thereby excluding from the benefits of full toleration not only all Deists and Atheists, but also Jews, Mahometans, and Socinians. Locke expressly lays down a cordon against the tolerance of Atheists and of Roman Catholics ; although in theory he maintains that the State is "a society of men only ordained for the preservation and promotion of civil advantages :"[1] a theory which would apparently condemn Lord Campbell's Act against the exhibition of immoral books and pictures, and all other legislation of that character. The weak points in Mill's essay on "Liberty" have been pointed out with singular force and vigour, both of thought and of expression, by Mr. Justice Stephen. But this able lawyer does, as we have intimated, in his turn shock and startle us. So strong is his conviction of the right of a dominant race to hold authority over a conquered country,—be it modern England over

---

[1] " Epistola de Tolerantiâ " (ed. Londini, 1765).

India, or ancient Rome over Palestine,—that he palliates, to say the very least, the conduct of Pontius Pilate in putting to death One in whom he had declared that he found no fault.

To return, however, to the special case before us. The aid of the civil authorities had, as we remarked, been sought by the adversaries of Priscillian. His friends looked in another direction. They sought ecclesiastical support from Rome. But the see of Rome was now occupied by a bishop who, if he had attained his position after a struggle which involved deeds of violence on the part of his adherents, at any rate used his power well and righteously. This was Damasus, famous in Church history for having employed as his private secretary, and cherished as an intimate friend, a man far more remarkable than himself,—the celebrated St. Jerome; and, perhaps, hardly less famous for the loving care and zeal with which he laboured in the renovation of the catacombs, a renovation of which the results are traceable down to the present day. Now, Damasus had been specially prominent as a champion of orthodoxy. He had taken part in the condemnation of Apollinaris; he had been zealous in the detection of concealed Arianism; and it was hardly probable that he would favour a form of heresy which would have proved no less fatal to the first elements of Christian truth than those he had already combated. From Damasus the Priscillianists obtained neither aid nor countenance.

They journeyed northward to the city of Milan; but Auxentius, the crypto-Arian bishop, who had thwarted the efforts of Hilary and of Martin, was dead.

His place was filled by one as unlike him in character
as in doctrine. In A.D. 374 Ambrose, though at that
time only a layman, had been raised, by popular
acclamation, to the bishopric of this important see.
But Ambrose was still less inclined than Damasus to
show favour to a heresy which would probably seem
to him worse than that Arianism which he was
then engaged in combating. Indeed, so completely
did the influence of the famous bishop of Milan tend
in the opposite direction, that we hear of several
Priscillians abjuring their errors in his presence.
Among these was a bishop named Symphosius,
from the province now called Galicia; also a Presbyter, named Dictinius, who afterwards became a
bishop in Asturia.

Meanwhile the opponents of Priscillian were not
idle, and in A.D. 384 we find their leader, Ithacius,
making a journey so far northward as to *Treviri*,
now known as Treves, and there requesting an
interview with the Emperor Maximus. Maximus
listened to the statements laid before him, and
ordered the convocation of a council at *Burdigala*
(Bordeaux) for the discussion of the question. That
this was a fair and legitimate step, thoroughly within
the lawful limits of imperial authority, was by this time
very generally admitted. The council met, and both
accuser and accused were present. But Priscillian,
instead of making any reply or defending his cause by
argument, declared his intention of appealing to the
emperor in person. This was what in later days
would have been called an Erastian proceeding. But
his opponents had already (at any rate, in practice)

made admissions in the same direction ; and the consciousness of the considerable amount of State interference which they had permitted, and indeed encouraged, apparently prevented them from raising objections which they felt would hardly be consistent. Accordingly Priscillian left Bordeaux for Treves, and his opponent, Ithacius, followed him.

Martin was also present at Treves. If we can trust Sulpicius, who is liberal in allowing to Priscillian the possession of the good qualities already mentioned, the progress of the contest not only brought out into strong relief the baser elements of his character, such as his extreme vanity, but developed other faults from which he had been hitherto believed exempt. We find two episcopal supporters of Priscillian, by name Instantius and Salvian, who travelled with him to Rome and Milan, accused, after their failure in these cities, of bribing imperial officers ; while their conduct in the course of the journey, more especially that of Priscillian, is represented as having been tainted with immorality. It is right to add that this historian is at the same time most emphatic in reprobation of the want of wisdom which had been displayed in Spain by the leaders of the orthodox school. A bishop of Merida, named Idatius, had, in the judgment of Sulpicius, been needlessly provocative, acting in a manner calculated to exasperate rather than to crush the heretical teachers. Moreover, both he and Ithacius had been most unwise in their appeals to the secular judges, seeking at their hands, and ultimately obtaining from the Emperor Gratian, decrees of banishment of the heretics from churches, from cities, and from all imperial territory. It was this revenge which induced Priscillian to make the tour which has been described.

Martin and Ithacius met at Treves. From the first the Spanish champion of orthodoxy was what the Italians would call not *simpatico* with Martin. Ithacius is represented as one who would call himself a practical man, and who harboured a feeling of dislike both to students and to ascetics. The Bishop of Tours had no claim to be ranked among the first-named of these classes ; but he unquestionably held a prominent place among the latter. The two prelates, while they agreed in recognizing in Priscillianism the character of deadly and pernicious heresy, yet differed widely respecting the proper mode of trial, and the kind of punishment which ought to be inflicted upon its author and abettors.

The nature and the results of these differences must be reserved for the succeeding chapter.

CHAPTER IX.

THE SENTENCE ON PRISCILLIAN AND HIS FOLLOWERS : ITS RESULTS.

THE dissent of Martin from the course which was being pursued by Ithacius was twofold. In the first place, the Bishop of Tours objected to the trial of a case of heresy before a secular tribunal such as was now sitting at Treves, and implored Ithacius not to proceed with his charges before this court.   Secondly, Martin used his influence with the Emperor Maximus to persuade him that if the case were pressed, no other punishment save that of excommunication should be inflicted.

Now excommunication is, in theory at least, a purely spiritual punishment. It was regarded in the primitive church as a power, similar indeed to that possessed by every independent club or corporation, of excluding persons from its society, just as it had the authority to admit them, but of course in this case a power rendered inexpressibly solemn, in consideration of the nature of the benefits conferred or withheld, and the source of the commandment for such action. To lose the pleasure and advantage arising from fellowship in the pursuit of amusement, literature, or art ; nay, even to undergo the dishonour (as the Greeks called it) involved in outlawry, or the deprivation of civil privileges, would be a punishment of which the effect upon the sufferer would end with this life. But exclusion from a divinely-constituted society, and consequently from means of grace, might include a loss which would reach beyond the grave. Such a power was, however, bestowed by our Lord upon the Church, and it was recognised and acted upon by the Apostles. The rulers of the Church were to bind and to loose ; to bind, by laying the hardened sinner and false teacher under the ban of exclusion from communion and from all ecclesiastical privileges ; to loose, by restoring to the penitent whatever had thus been taken away. Where their sentence was sincere, and not the result of passion or hypocrisy, it was to avail not only before men, but before God. If it be urged, that the great Head of the Church would hardly have meant to bestow upon it a gift so capable of perversion by the narrowness or short-sightedness of men, it must be replied that such an objection would equally apply to the possible defects, corruptions, and errors of preaching. Both dangers were doubtless alike foreseen. The treasure is in earthen vessels : the human instruments appointed to carry out a divine purpose will but too often fail. But this is part of the necessity of the condition of a church militant : and no failures and shortcomings will avail to counteract the far greater blessings arising out of these ordinances.

In the hand of Apostles they were safe. Gifted with extraordinary powers of knowledge and insight, an Apostle could say, as regards preaching, that he had not shrunk from declaring unto the flocks under his charge the whole counsel of God. Even when absent in body he would be present in spirit, and join with a local Church in excommunicating a grievous and scandalous offender. He could also see when it was fitting to modify a sentence, that the guilty one might not be swallowed up with overmuch sorrow. He could discern the proper measure of chastisement, which should benefit, not only the culprit, but the community at large. It is possible that Apostles may have also been endowed with an exceptional power of chastisement, distinct from excommunication, although on necessary occasions combined with it.[1]

Such fulness of wisdom and courage in preaching, such tact and judgment in the enforcement of discipline, could hardly be looked for in the ordinary course of God's providence, even in the divinely-constituted society which He Himself had founded, and of which His son is in His human nature the appointed Head. There came a day in the rolling years when this power of excommunication was grievously abused, when the sentence was often inflicted for purely temporal offences. Partly as a natural result of such abuse, partly from the divisions of Christendom and the changed condition of society, the terror which excommunication once carried with it is in our time all but unknown. And yet not only in the primitive church, but often also in the middle ages, it has been an instrument of great value for society. This is now fully admitted by

[1] Acts xx. 20, 26, 27; 1 Cor. v. 1–5; 2 Cor. ii. 5–11; 1 Tim. i. 19, 20.

writers who view the matter from an extraneous
position. We must be content to mention Michelet, in
his History of France, and his sympathetic reviewer
J. S. Mill. Both observe how needful it was in an age
when the great of the earth were all but unrestrained
by public opinion, that there should be some power
which could say to such, "You shall not set yourself
above the moral law." The Church was the only
power that was then capable of such action, and in
a multitude of instances the power was wielded
efficiently and well.

Ought she, endowed as she was with that spiritual
power, to have craved at the hands of temporal
authority the use of the civil sword?—and if so, within
what limits?

That civil punishment for spiritual offences was
known to heathendom and outside the Mosaic law, is
undeniable. Blasphemy, the introduction of strange
rites, atheism, betrayal of sacred mysteries, and even
slight insults to consecrated groves or temples, were,
in most Grecian states, capital offences. This was no
mere theory. Æsop, the writer of fables, was thrown
down the crag of Hyampe for blasphemy; and though
it seems to have been subsequently recognized as a
mistaken decision as regards the person, the principle
remained uncondemned. The poet Æschylus incurred
great danger for an accidental revelation of something
in the Eleusinian mysteries. The sculptor Phidias
died in prison, into which he had been thrown for
introducing his own likeness and that of Pericles on
a shield of Pallas. Alleged impiety was one of the
charges under which Socrates was condemned to

death. These cases, with many more, occur between B.C. 550–400.

In Holy Scripture we find the book of Job recognizing nature-worship and (by implication) denial of the true God as an offence to be punished by the judge; and the Mosaic law punished with death the introduction of idolatry, blasphemy, and irreverence towards parents.[1] A special judgment of the Almighty visited with death the first great offence committed against the Holy Spirit in the infant Church at Jerusalem.

At the moment when we are writing there is a strong feeling abroad that the members of any religious community which is tolerated by the State ought to be protected from outrage and insult. Indeed, where such protection is not granted, there is a real risk of what is commonly known as lynch law being executed upon the offenders. Such was the danger incurred by Thos. Pooley some years ago, when he persisted in writing obnoxious blasphemies upon a public gate. Such would probably be the peril incurred by the men who, during the present year [1883], have been sentenced to imprisonment.[2]

---

[1] Deut. xiii. 6–10; xvii. 2–5; xxi. 18–21; Leviticus xxiv. 10–16.

[2] "What we really punish by the law of blasphemous libel is an offence against public decency, and until we have other means of dealing with that nuisance we need not be alarmed by outcries about danger to free speech. In respect of religion, there is no conceivable latitude of view in which a man may not indulge unmolested so long as he does not wantonly outrage the feelings of others, whose rights are as much entitled to consideration as his own. The law of blasphemy, as laid down by

It need hardly be said that for long ages the general sentiment of Christendom went far beyond this. The punishment of heresy by death was assumed as almost an axiom by some of the holiest and best of men. St. Louis, king of France, thought the immediate answer of a layman to a gainsaying Jew lay in the sword. St. Ferdinand of Spain is praised in the Roman Breviary for having taken faggots with his own hands to burn heretics. The execution of Servetus by Calvin met with approval from all the foreign Reformers, including even the mild Melancthon. John Knox, in a conversation with Maitland, asserted most explicitly the duty of putting idolaters to death ; and among idolaters he included all Roman Catholics. " Nothing," says Hallam, " can be more sanguinary than the Reformer's spirit in this remarkable interview. St. Dominic could not have surpassed him." Latimer, who himself suffered with such effective courage, had preached the sermon at the burning by a slow fire of Friar Forest, confessor to Queen Catharine. In like manner Cranmer and Ridley were largely responsible for the similar death inflicted upon Joan Bocher for Arianism. Between 1628 and 1654, some twenty

Mr. Justice North, and as practically applied in this country during the present century, is a law for the protection of liberty." —*Times* of March 6th, 1883, in reference to the case of G. W. Foote. It has been said that in this case the caricatures relating to the life of Christ our Lord were so disgusting and offensive as to blanch the cheeks of many whose eyes they met ; and that it is highly probable that the publishers would have been punished in many Mohammedan countries, where *Issa Ben Mariam* (Jesus Son of Mary) is at least reverenced as a great prophet.

Roman Catholic priests suffered capitally through the condemnation of the British Parliament ; and these years, it must be remembered, include a period during which the Parliament was practically the sovereign power. Robertson is probably right when he says of the Reformers of the sixteenth century, that "to their followers, and perhaps to their opponents, it would have appeared a symptom of diffidence in the goodness of their cause, or an acknowledgment that it was not well founded if they had not employed in its defence all those means which it was supposed truth had a right to employ."[1]

But during the last century and a half it has occurred to many Christians to inquire whether the capital punishment for blasphemy or heresy, however consonant to the spirit of the elder dispensation, is not opposed to the general tone of our Lord's teaching and example. The death of Ananias and Sapphira, being a supernatural judgment, does not carry with it a proof that the penalty of death, when naturally inflicted, is right. Even that case was to be rare and exceptional. "Ye know not what spirit ye are of," is the rebuke administered to Apostles who would fain have called down fire from heaven.[2] Few among members of reformed communions would venture to defend it ; and one of the most eloquent of modern protests against executions for opinion was uttered by a Roman Catholic layman, the late Count of Montalembert.

[1] Life of Charles V., cited in Smyth's "Lectures on Modern History," vol. i., Lect. x.

[2] St. Luke ix. 51-55. The shortened reading adopted in the Revised Version does not affect the general sense.

As, however, every such assertion by a layman
has hitherto been condemned by the ecclesiastical
authorities of the Church of Rome, we must suppose
that its lawfulness is still maintained by that communion. This circumstance lends a living interest to
the question concerning the treatment of Priscillian
and his followers.

The demands upon Martin's time were many and
varied. His presence was needed in other parts of
Gaul. So long as he had remained at Treves, the
judicial inquiry into the case was put off. Before his
departure Martin, according to Sulpicius, succeeded
by his great influence in obtaining a promise from the
Emperor Maximus that no capital punishment should
be inflicted upon the accused ; but directly Martin
disappeared from the scene, two bishops, named
respectively Magnus and Rufus, gained the ear of the
emperor and turned him aside from the gentler
counsels which had hitherto prevailed. Maximus
submitted the case to the judgment of a layman, the prefect Evodius, a man of high character,
with the reputation of being a just judge, but with a
leaning towards sternness and severity. | Priscillian
and his followers were tried upon the charges not
only of false doctrine, but likewise of immoral conduct in the very meetings which they ostensibly con-
vened for prayer. Evodius pronounced them to be
guilty on both counts, and sent them back to prison
until the emperor could take further action. On the
decision of the prefect reaching the palace, Maximus
straightway pronounced a capital sentence.| Among
those involved in this condemnation was one Latro-

nianus, and a lady named Euchrocia, wife of the
orator Delphidius. Meanwhile, another female disciple of Priscillian, named Urbica, had proved so
outspoken in what seemed to the people of Bordeaux
rank impiety, that the mob of that city arose and stoned
her to death. / Two formerly orthodox clergy named
Felicissimus and Armenius, who had but recently
revolted and joined Priscillian, were included in the
sentence, as was also one Asarinus, and a deacon
named Aurelius. ιTwo others, Instantius and Tiberian,
were exiled to the Scilly Islands off the coast of
Cornwall. Three of inferior position turned informers
before the application of that torture, which (sad to
say) was applied to the rest of the accused.

It will be seen presently in what form a protest
against the entire proceeding came from another
quarter not less eminent than that which has been
implied. For the present let it suffice to observe
that on the first occasion of a heretic being put to
death,[1] distinct and solemn protests proceeded from

---

[1] The opinion that to inflict death for heresy is wrong seems
to have been condemned implicitly, to say the least, by the
late Pope Pius IX. It is also, we presume, implicitly censured in the following words by Cardinal Newman, concerning
the Church of Rome :—"All she asks is an open field and freedom to act. She asks no patronage from the civil power; in
former times and places she has asked it ; and, as Protestantism
also, has availed herself of the civil sword. It is true she did so,
because in certain ages it has been the acknowledged mode of
acting, the most expeditious [!] *and open at the time to no objection*, and because, where she has done so, *the people clamoured
for it* [!] and did it in advance of her; but her history shows
she needed it not, for she has extended and flourished without

two of the most saintly and influential prelates of
their age,—Martin of Tours and Ambrose of Milan ;
that similar protests were made by two local councils
held respectively at Milan and Turin, the last-named receiving the approbation of the then bishop of Rome,
Pope Siricius ; that of the bishops most prominent in
procuring the sentence, two, Ithacius and Ursacius,
were subsequently (in the reign of Theodosius and
Valentinian) excommunicated and sent into exile ;
while a third, Nardacius, though less guilty, voluntarily
for a time resigned his see ; and that the sentence on
Priscillian and his adherents proved in its results a
most entire failure. This last-named feature of the
case cannot be stated more emphatically than in the
actual words of Sulpicius, with which, in an almost

it."—"Discourses to Mixed Congregations," p. 250. The
Dublin Review directly censured M. de Montalembert. It
seems fair to add that Coleridge was inclined to consider capital
punishment for the promulgation of false and dangerous opinions
lawful, though unwise. The author of "John Inglesant" regards
it as a logical sequence from the Roman Catholic doctrine ; as
did also Arthur Hallam, who, however, believed that all Monotheism, especially such Monotheism as the Christian, was a
source of unavoidable persecution ("Remains," p. 279). Mr.
Lecky goes further and maintains that a belief in *any* dogma
whatever involves persecution. A short but highly suggestive
paper on the subject of Persecution was contributed to the
Scottish Guardian (Aberdeen : Brown), for August, 1866, by the
Rev. A. Alfred Plummer, now Master of University College,
Durham.   Of anti-Christian intolerance it is needless to speak.
It is attested by the annals of Christendom during the Church's
first three hundred years of existence ; by the history of France
—to name one country only—during the great Revolution,
which began in 1789 ; and by events occurring in the years
1870 and 1883.

literal translation, we must conclude the present portion of our narrative :—

" But by the death of Priscillian the heresy, of which he had been the author and promulgator, was not merely unrepressed, but strengthened and more widely propagated. For his adherents, who had previously honoured him as a saint, subsequently began to cherish his memory as that of a martyr. The bodies of the slain were carried back to Spain, and their obsequies were grandly celebrated. Nay, it was even reckoned a mark of the deepest piety to swear by Priscillian. Among our fellow-Christians in that land an unceasing war and discord prevailed ; and for the space of fifteen years the dire agitation of the dissensions thence arising remained utterly unchecked."

Sulpicius adds that the saddest feature of all was the display of the turmoil and confusion wrought by the discord between the bishops (the majority of whom he taxes with faulty conduct of every kind), and the disgrace and scorn that thus fell upon God's people at large, and especially on the best among them.

Assuredly it does not look as if the use of the civil sword against heresy was, in the fourth century, considered to be open to no objection.

CHAPTER X.

CONCLUSION.

THE issue of the affair of the Priscillianists was destined to affect the remainder of Martin's career. The execution had taken place in A.D. 385 ; and both Martin and Ambrose, in protesting against it, announced their determination to decline all communion with the bishops who had been instrumental in procuring the sentence. The resolution of each was subsequently tested, but in a different manner and with different results.

Two years after the execution (that is to say, in A.D. 387), Ambrose paid a visit to Treves. His object was to recover the body of the Emperor Gratian, who had been assassinated ; but he found it to be a condition of success that he should communicate with the prelates whose society he had abjured. This price for such an object Ambrose was determined not to pay. Accordingly he adhered to his resolve, and departed.

But meanwhile Martin also had made another journey to Treves. He had come, not to supplicate for the restoration of a corpse, but to intercede for the pardon of some officers who, having adhered to Gratian, were under sentence of capital punishment. Maximus, who had continued to protect Ithacius and his friends, made the condition of success the same

for Martin as for Ambrose ; but there is, of course, a
wide difference between failure in obtaining the body
of the dead, with a view to honourable interment,
and want of success in securing the safety of the
living.   Nor did the impending fate of Count Narses
and of Leucadius (two prominent supporters of ·
Gratian) alone affect the resolves of Martin.   A new
commission, armed with the right of the sword, was
about to start for Spain.   There was every reason
to fear that no great discernment would be exercised,
and that some excellent Christians, especially if they
looked pale and ascetic, would unjustly suffer as
Priscillianists.   But Martin was anxious, even apart
from this danger, to free the heretics themselves from
further temporal molestation.

The number of bishops then present at Treves,
was considerable ; for, the see being vacant, there
was a gathering for the purpose of consecrating a
successor to the late bishop.   The character of the
person chosen, by name Felix, was unexceptionable ;
and for Martin to take part in such a function would,
under ordinary circumstances, have been a matter of
course.   But the bishops congregated at Treves had,
with one exception, communicated with the Ithacians,
and were held to have thereby given their sanction to
the execution of the Priscillianists.   They were profoundly conscious of the immense influence exercised
by Martin ; and, after having vainly attempted to
prevent his arrival at the seat of the court, they
vehemently implored the emperor to use his influence
with this much-dreaded antagonist.   If, they argued,
Theognistus (the one recalcitrant bishop) obtained the

public sanction of the Bishop of Tours for his conduct, the punishment of Priscillian would prove to
have been utterly unprofitable and barren of result.

Maximus sympathised with the bishops and sent
for Martin. The emperor urged that Priscillian had
been justly condemned by regular legal proceedings,
quite apart from any episcopal persecutions; that
Theognistus stood alone, and was not influenced by
really good motives; and that a very recent synod
held at Treves had thoroughly absolved Ithacius.
All this was laid before Martin with much gentleness;
but when no impression had been made, Maximus
became angry and retired. His next step was to
appoint executioners for the political prisoners.

This proceeding, although he heard of it in the
night-time, at once brought Martin back to the
palace. He promised to communicate, provided that
the condemned officers were spared, and that the
commission, which had started from Spain, was recalled. The emperor consented, and Martin communicated with the assembled episcopate; they, not
unnaturally, requested his signature as a confirmation
of his conduct; but to this request, it is not obvious
on what ground, their brother prelate absolutely
refused consent.

On the next day Martin departed from Treves in
a mournful and agitated frame of mind. Not far
from the city lay in those days a vast forest, named
Andethanna. Martin let his companions go onward
for a space, while he sat down and revolved in his
mind the arguments for and against even this momen-
tary consent to a communion with brethren whom he

regarded as wrong-doers. An angel, he believed, descended and stood beside him, and addressed him ⋏ to this effect :—"Martin, thou art smitten with compunction, but no other way of escape was left. Seek fresh grace, renew thy firmness, lest thou risk the loss not of mere reputation, but of salvation itself." From that time, so the Bishop of Tours told his friends, he was conscious of a loss of power when he tried to exorcise the possessed. He did not absolutely fail, but the cure was less rapid and complete than heretofore ; though, according to his biographer, this diminution of success was only temporary. Not only did he abstain from any further act of communion with the Ithacians, but for the remainder of his life,—that is to say, for at least eleven, possibly for sixteen,[1] years,—he kept aloof from all assemblages of bishops.

A devout French historian, the Abbé Velly, has said : "There is much rashness in condemning certain actions of saints ; we ought to be what they have been, in order to judge aright what they have done." It is certainly well (especially in an age when intellect often counts for so much, and humility and conscience for so little) to meditate upon such a maxim as this ; and yet it may be pressed too far. Men of great holiness have made mistakes, and we must not abnegate our right of judgment on their conduct. It surely need not be any lack of appre-

---

[1] Sixteen years is the ordinary reading of the passage (Sulpicius, "Dialogus," iii., cap. 15). The conjecture of a great authority, Fynes Clinton, in favour of eleven (*undecim* for *sedecim*) would remove some difficulties of chronology.

ciation of Martin's many claims to admiration to say that a bishop, who for long years forsakes all gatherings of his brethren, is neglecting a most important portion of the duties appertaining to his sacred office. The very circumstance of the entanglement might have taught him wariness for the future. As it was, others who were trying in synods to advance the Church's work must have lost the powerful aid and counsel which Martin's sanctified experience might have afforded them.

But in all other respects Martin continued his labours as an evangelizer of Gaul to the very close of his long life, which seems to have extended to at least 81 years (A.D. 316–397). Many visited him during these later days that they might learn something from his words and examples. Among these is said to have been St. Patrick, who (according to one of the dubious narratives concerning him) was a nephew of St. Martin, being the son of St. Martin's sister, Conkessa. But the popular accounts of St. Patrick are not earlier than the ninth century.[1]

One negative feature of his career seems to have struck even ultramontane critics. Neither for approbation of his work nor for solution of his difficulties did Martin ever seem to have dreamed of any application to Rome.[2] His sole journey thither, of which we have any record, was that already mentioned,

[1] Skene's Introduction to the Dean of Lismore's book, p. lxxiii. (cited by Bishop Forbes, of Brechin, in the "Kalendars of Scottish Saints," p. 433, Edinburgh, 1872).
[2] See, for example, the very uncritical article in the *Dublin Review* for January, 1883, on St. Martin and St. Patrick.

when he hoped to find there his friend Hilary of Poitiers. Having failed in his object, he at once started northward.

The close of Martin's life was pious and edifying. He thought, indeed, that the ancient enemy of souls, against whose kingdom he had warred so earnestly, appeared to him once more ; but it was a vision only to be defied and dismissed. His funeral is said to have been attended by two thousand monks. Of his wide-spread celebrity, even in the fourth and fifth centuries, we have many testimonies. The Greek historian, Sozomen, devotes a brief chapter to his career. His name was famous in Southern Italy at the time of his decease ; and the booksellers at Rome declared that no works were in greater demand than the biography and dialogues concerning him, which were written by his friend Sulpicius. In England twenty-eight churches have been dedicated to his memory, that of Canterbury being among the oldest in Britain. Looking northward, we find the earliest missionary to Scotland, St. Ninian, dedicating in Martin's name the first stone church erected in that country ; namely, *Candida Casa* in Galloway. Scotland to this day recognizes the celebrity of this Saint by making the anniversary of his death (the eleventh of November [1]) one of its term days ; and, before the Reformation, the earls of Douglas figured in the long list of ecclesiastical and lay dignitaries who were honorary canons of his abbey near the city of Tours. The list included the patriarch of

---

[1] The exact date is probably a little earlier in the month, but the eleventh has been long kept as the day.

Jerusalem, the archbishop of Cologne, the counts of
Flanders, Dunois, and Angoulême; and (from the
time of Charles the Bald, who died A:D. 877) the
king of France, as its abbot and first canon. It was
secularized in the seventh century. Just at the close
of the tenth century, the first Christian king of
Norway, Olaf Tryggvesen, selected Martin to be the
patron saint of that kingdom. These are only a few
specimens of the honours paid to his memory.[1] Our
limits forbid a longer enumeration. But we must
not omit to mention that his name is contained in
the liturgy of St. Gregory as that of a confessor for
the faith, in company with Linus, Cletus, Hilary,
Augustine, and thirteen others.

There is a copious French bibliography connected
with the name of St. Martin. The secular historians
of the country usually do him justice, Michelet
being specially appreciative. Sismondi is less favourable, but then he is seldom just to pre-Reformation
Christianity, having written before the revolution
of thought brought about by Thierry, Vogt, and
others, above all by Guizot. But, although the
abundance of memoirs and notices testifies to the
depth of the impress made by the Bishop of Tours, it
may be questioned whether these avail to explain the
real difficulty connected with his memory and career.

The difficulty is this, that the impression made by
Martin looks, to the ordinary observer, out of all
proportion to the record of his life. In the case of

[1] The learned Roman Catholic hagiologist, Alban Butler,
mentions several more; admitting, however, that an exhaustive
list would require a volume.

a large number of the prominent figures in Church history, we can point to the books which they wrote, the councils at which they presided or assisted, the heresies which they combated, the eloquence of their sermons, the interest of their correspondence, their contributions to the formation of doctrine, or to the interpretation of Holy Scripture. In the case of Martin all these features are lacking ; and yet Martin remains undeniably the one prelate who has made the deepest impression upon the heart and imagination of France, and of a large part of Christendom beyond the limits of his adopted country.

That, after all allowance for a vast amount of credulous exaggeration, it may remain true that the work of this famous missionary was frequently aided by supernatural answers to prayer, can be, at best, but a partial solution of the problem. Similar claims may be made for other missionaries, who nevertheless fall far short of the celebrity won by Martin. Something is no doubt due to the elegant Latinity and compressed brevity of Sulpicius ; and perhaps still more to a charm of manner which, though described by his biographer, may have been handed down by tradition in many quarters which written records failed to penetrate. Contemporaries, and others no less loyal and even successful in their service than Martin, may remain unknown for want of narratives, or because they lacked that charm of personal fascination.

It is admitted, even by leading Roman Catholics of this century,—we have already mentioned Möhler and the Duc de Broglie,—that many of the stories related concerning the hermits in the desert must be regarded as "external representations, under a living and sensible form, of the struggle of the Christian soul against passion and sin." M. de Broglie, whose words we have just quoted, proceeds to liken them to Bunyan's famous allegory, "The Pilgrim's Progress." The same principle of interpretation is applicable to a large number of the marvels related concerning Martin; and lessons may be derived from them, even by those who may be inclined to suppose that the details of the story may represent only a subjective conviction, as well as by those who regard them as objectively true. A great writer, who has made the third and fourth centuries of the Church's history the object of his most special studies, some forty years ago gave us a specimen of such treatment. Its interest and beauty are such, that with it we may well conclude.

Sulpicius relates that the Evil One once appeared to Martin as he was praying in his cell. Satan was clad in royal robes, with a diadem of gems and gold on his head, and displayed a calm expression and a face of joy. After a long silence, on both sides, the visitor announced himself as Christ, who was thus honouring his host by visiting him before His second advent, which was at hand. Hesitation on Martin's part was met by renewed assertion. But by this time the real nature of the speaker had been revealed to Martin, and he declared that he would believe in the coming of his Lord when he saw Him in the dress and form in which He suffered, and displaying the wounds inflicted on the cross.

The following is the comment of the then vicar of
St. Mary's, Oxford :—" The application of this vision
to Martin's age is obvious : I suppose it means in
this day, that Christ comes not in pride of intellect
or reputation for philosophy.   These are the glittering
robes in which Satan is now arraying.   Many spirits
are abroad, more are issuing from the pit; the
credentials which they display are the precious
gifts of mind, beauty, richness, depth, originality.
*Christian, look hard at them with Martin in silence,
and ask them for the print of the nails.*" [1]

The years which have elapsed since these words
were published have in no wise lessened, nay, surely
have greatly intensified, our need of the warning
which they utter.   May we all have grace to lay
them to heart, in so far as they tend to promote our
highest and eternal welfare !

[1] " Church of the Fathers," by John Henry Newman.

INDEX.

---

[1] Jerome, however, questions Hilary's thorough mastery of the Greek language.

[1] Valentinian, though prejudiced against Martin by his Arian empress, became friendly to him during their brief intercourse.

THE END.

WYMAN AND SONS, PRINTERS, GREAT QUEEN STREET, LONDON, W.C.

www.ingramcontent.com/pod-product-compliance
Lightning Source LLC
Chambersburg PA
CBHW030631030726
47497CB00006B/1740